BLACK & DECKER
HOME IMPROVEMENT LIBRARY

Great Decks
& Furnishings

A Step-by-Step Guide

CREATIVE
PUBLISHING
international

www.howtobookstore.com

Credits

Editorial Director: Bryan Trandem
Associate Creative Director: Tim Himsel
Managing Editor: Jennifer Caliandro
Lead Editor: Richard Steven
Editors: Craig Gelderman, Karl Larson,
   Danny London
Copy Editor: Janice Cauley
Technical Photo Editors: John Fletcher,
   Joel Schmarje
Senior Art Director: Kevin Walton
Mac Designers: Eileen Bovard, Phyllis Lee,
   Jon Simpson, Brad Webster
Project Manager: Tracy Stanley
Contributing Draftsman: John T. Drigot
Illustrator: Mike Kohlrusch

Vice President of Photography & Production:
   Jim Bindas
Studio Services Manager: Marcia Chambers
Photo Services Coordinator: Carol Osterhus
Photographers: Doug Deutscher,
   Rebecca Schmitt, Chuck Nields,
   Andrea Rugg
Scene Shop Carpenters: Troy Johnson,
   Greg Wallace
Production Manager: Stasia Dorn
Purchasing Manager: Dave Austad

Special thanks to: P & M Cedar Products, Inc.,
Redding, CA and Canton Lumber, Brooklyn Park,
MN for providing cedar wood products.

Special thanks to Tim Anderson, Clayton Bennett,
and Tim Canfield, who reviewed various aspects
of the manuscript and made valuable suggestions.

Copyright ©1998 Creative Publishing International
5900 Green Oak Drive
Minnetonka, MN 55343
1-800-328-3895
www.howtobookstore.com
Printed in U.S.A.
10 9 8 7 6 5 4 3

President/CEO: David D. Murphy
VP/Retail Sales & Marketing: Kevin Haas

Created by: The Editors of Creative
Publishing International in cooperation
with Black & Decker. Black & Decker
is a trademark of the Black & Decker
Corporation and is used under license.

Library of Congress Cataloging-in-Publication Data

Great decks and furnishings : a step-by-step guide.
       p.   cm. -- (Portable workshop)
    "Black & Decker."
    "Basic wood projects with portable power tools."
    Includes index.
    ISBN 0-86573-487-9 (soft cover)
    1. Decks (Architecture, Domestic)--Design and construction--
Amateurs' manuals. 2. Outdoor furniture. I. Cowles Creative
Publishing. II. Black & Decker Corporation (Towson, Md.)
III. Series.
TX739.H657 1998
690'.893--dc21   98-19927

Contents

Introduction

A deck can be the perfect place to entertain guests, to eat a meal or relax at the end of a long day. A deck offers a distinctive space where you can enjoy the outdoors in comfort. A deck not only enhances a home's livability, but can also increase a home's dollar value. It's for these reasons that deck building is one of the most popular home improvements today.

It may surprise you that although decks offer so many benefits, building one is within the capabilities of most do-it-yourselfers. With the right plans, the proper tools and some free time, you can build a deck that you'll enjoy for many years.

Inside *Great Decks & Furnishings: A Step-by-Step Guide,* you'll find seven original deck plans. Each plan is unique, so you'll be able to choose one that is right for your home.

Each plan contains easy-to-follow instructions that will guide you, from sinking the first footing to drilling the final lag screw. And each plan comes with a comprehensive list of building materials, something do-it-yourselfers have come to expect from Black & Decker books.

While typical deck books provide only computerized drawings of decks, each plan in *Great Decks & Furnishings* contains a materials list, detailed technical drawings and clear, color photographs of important construction steps.

To make your work even easier, each plan contains valuable, clearly explained tips and pointers from the experts.

On the following pages, we've provided an informative materials and hardware guide to help you select the proper lumber and parts, guidance on the best way to ensure approval from a building inspector and detailed photographs identifying all the tools you'll need.

The final chapter, "Modifying a Deck Design," offers the guidance you'll need should you decide to change the height or shape of your deck or alter the design to accommodate distinctive landscape features, utilities or aesthetic considerations.

The handy "Appendix" at the end of the book includes a glossary and an easy-to-read lumber chart.

We've also included several plans for deck furnishings and accessories, including a beautiful cedar arbor and a handsome flower planter, that will add custom charm to your deck.

With all this, it's clear that *Great Decks & Furnishings* will be a great addition to your library. We hope you'll use it to make a great addition to your home.

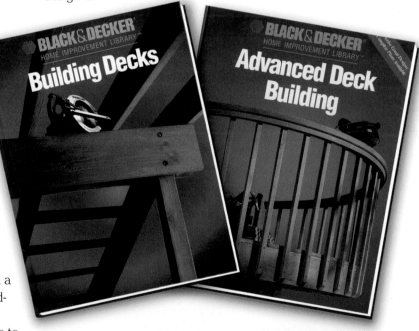

ADDITIONAL RESOURCES

Other great deck books from the Black & Decker® Home Improvement Library™ include Building Decks, *and* Advanced Deck Building, *published by Creative Publishing International. For deck ideas and designs consult* A Portfolio of Deck Ideas, *also from Creative Publishing International.* Outdoor Wood Furnishings, *may be of interest to anyone who wants to spruce up a deck with dimensional lumber furniture.*

Lumber

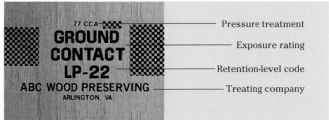

Pressure-treated lumber stamps list the type of preservative and the chemical retention level, as well as the exposure rating and the name and location of the treating company.

Cedar grade stamps list the mill number, moisture content, species, lumber grade and membership association. Western red cedar (WRC) or incense cedar (INC) for decks should be heartwood (HEART) with a maximum moisture content of 15% (MC 15).

When constructing a deck, select a wood that is not prone to rot or insect attack. Three types are recommended: heart cedar, heart redwood and pressure-treated lumber.

The heartwood of cedar and redwood is highly resistant to decay; the sapwood is not, and must be treated with a preservative when used for outdoor structures.

Because cedar and redwood are somewhat expensive, many deck builders use these woods only on the visible parts of decks and use less expensive pressure-treated lumber, with its telltale green tint, on less visible parts. The preservatives in pressure-treated wood provide a high resistance to decay. But because the chemicals used in the process are toxic, you must wear eye protection, a particle mask and

gloves, and cover your skin when working with pressure-treated lumber. Further, the Building Code may require you to dispose of waste lumber as if it were a hazardous material.

Many deck builders seal the ends of all boards, even if they are pressure-treated, to ensure that the end grain doesn't rot.

When selecting wood for your deck, inspect the lumber for warping and twisting. Any lumber for structural parts of the deck should be free of knots. Also inspect the end grain. Lumber with a vertical grain will cup less as it ages.

The materials lists for the plans in this book include a waste allowance of 10 to 15%.

Store lumber a few inches off the ground and use blocks between each row to ensure air flow. Keep the wood covered with a waterproof tarp.

LUMBER ALTERNATIVES

Redwood, cedar and pressure-treated boards are popular for deck building because of their resistance to decay. However, they have environmental drawbacks. Redwood and cedar trees are relatively scarce, and conventional CCA (chromated copper arsenate) pressure treatment leaves a residue on boards that can result in harmful runoff.

Lumberyards are now offering several alternatives. Many now offer ACQ-treated wood, which is effective against rot, decay and termite attack, but uses chemicals that are less harmful than CCA.

Wood/polymer composites are another option. They look like wood—but with a more uniform, less grainy, appearance—and are made of recycled plastics and waste wood. Composites can be used for decking and other nonstructural components. They also offer some advantages over wood since they will not rot or crack and are highly resistant to moisture, insects and ultraviolet rays.

Materials & Hardware

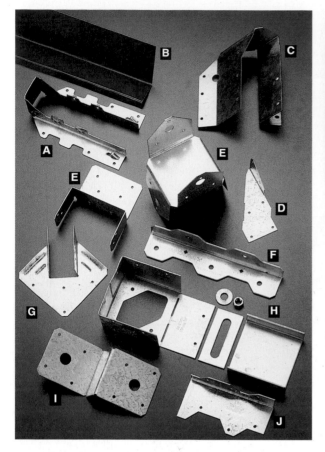

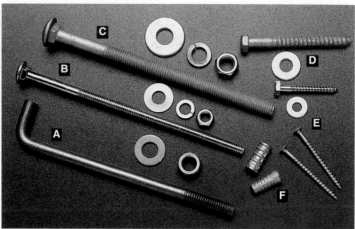

(Above photo) Deck fasteners include: J-bolt with nut and washer (A), carriage bolts with washers and nuts (B, C), galvanized lag screws and washers (D), corrosion-resistant deck screw (E), masonry anchor (F).

(Left photo) Metal connectors used in deck building include: joist hanger (A), flashing (B), angled joist hanger (C), rafter tie (D), post-beam caps (E), stair cleat (F), H-fit joist ties (G), post anchor with washer and pedestal (H), joist tie (I), angle bracket (J).

Use the deck plans and elevations to make a complete list of the items you will need.

Most supplies for building a deck are available at lumberyards or home improvement centers. Full-service lumber-yards have a complete selection of building materials, but prices may be higher than those at home improvement centers. The quality of lumber at home centers can vary, so inspect the wood and hand-pick the pieces you want.

Order top-quality hardware, caulks, wood sealers and stains. Save money on high-quality nails, screws and other hardware by buying in bulk.

Concrete is a mixture of one part portland cement, two parts sand and three parts coarse gravel. Buy concrete in premixed bags for smaller jobs. If a lot of concrete is called for, consider renting a power mixer, which can blend large quantities of cement, gravel, sand and water quickly.

Tools

When shopping for power tools, choose tools that are double-insulated, have a comfortable grip and have heavy-duty motors. Some of the more expensive tools, such as a power miter box and reciprocating saw, may be available at tool rental outlets.

Most of the hand tools needed to build a deck are found in an average do-it-yourselfer's workshop. In all likelihood, the only tools you will need to purchase are the specialized tools necessary for masonry work. Buy quality tools that have a comfortable handle, are well balanced and feel sturdy. Although often more expensive, a well-made tool is a good investment. It will last far longer than a cheap tool and make your project easier and more enjoyable.

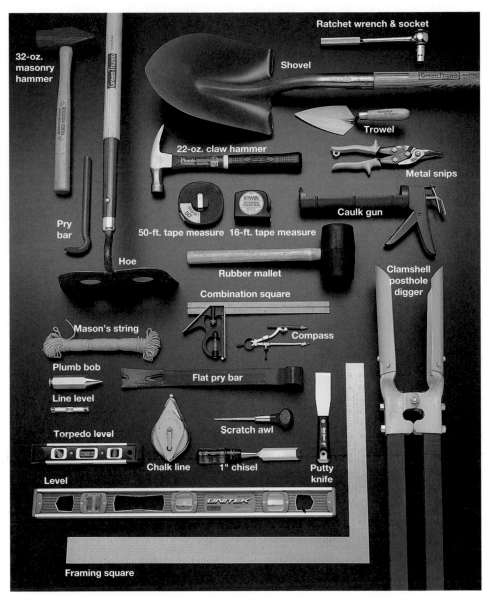

Hand tools for deck building should have heavy-duty construction. Metal tools should be made from high-carbon steel with smoothly finished surfaces. Buy quality hand tools that are well balanced and have tight, comfortable molded handles.

The power tools you will find useful to complete a project include power miter saw (A), 14.4-volt cordless trim saw with a 5⅜"-blade (B), reciprocating saw with 6" and 8" blades (C), ⅜" drill and bits (D), jig saw (E), and ½" hammer drill and bits (F).

Building Officials & Codes

In most regions, you must have your plans reviewed and approved by a building official if your deck is attached to a permanent structure or if it is more than 30" high. The building official makes sure that your planned deck meets Building Code requirements for safe construction.

Since Code regulations vary from area to area, check with the building inspection division of your city government before you build your project. A valuable source of planning information, the building official may provide you with a free information sheet outlining relevant requirements. In regions with cold winters, for example, Code generally requires footings to be sunk below the frost line.

Once you have chosen plans for your deck, return to the building inspections office and have the official review them. If your plans meet Code, you will be issued a building permit, usually for a small fee.

Regulations may require that a field inspector review the deck at specified stages in the building process. If so, make sure to comply with the review schedule.

Plan-approval Checklist

When the building official reviews your deck plans, he or she will look for the following details. Make sure your plan drawings include this information when you visit the building inspection office to apply for a permit.

- Overall size of the deck.
- Deck's position relative to buildings and property lines.
- Location of all beams and posts.
- Size and on-center (OC) spacing of joists.
- Thickness of decking boards.
- Height of the deck above the ground.
- Detailed drawings of joinery methods for all structural members of the deck.
- Type of soil that will support the concrete post footings: sand, gravel or clay.
- Species of wood you will use.
- Types of metal connectors and other hardware you plan to use when constructing your deck.

Understanding & Working with Plans

Our step-by-step plans should provide you with almost everything you need to know to build a deck. If you follow them correctly, you will have a deck that provides hours of enjoyment, summer after summer.

When working with a plan, become familiar with common symbols and conventions before beginning the project. As you prepare to cut lumber, take the time to confirm the exact measurements of all the cuts.

Though a step-by-step plan provides much of the information needed to build a great deck, it is still up to you to evaluate the labor and costs involved. Deck costs vary widely depending on size and materials.

The plans in this book should conform with the Building Code in your area, but you still need to get approval from your local building inspector.

Before setting an appointment with a building inspector, make a photocopy of your plan. Write down any relevant details about your house, the immediate area around the deck, the grade of the site where the deck will stand and any changes you plan on making to the materials list.

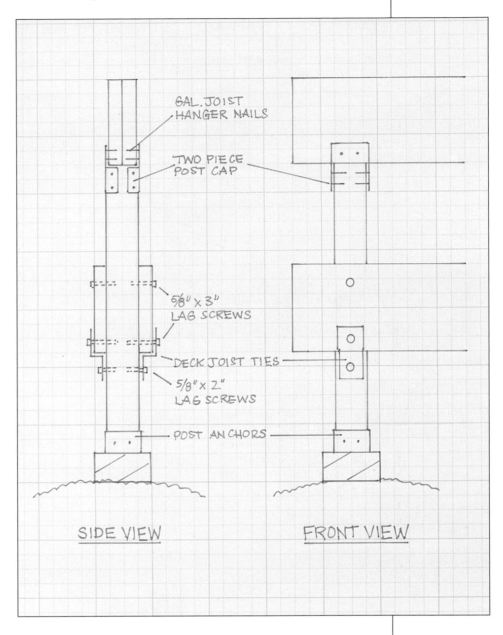

NOTICE TO READERS

This book provides useful instructions, but we cannot anticipate all of your working conditions or the characteristics of your materials and tools. For safety, you should use caution, care and good judgment when following the procedures described in this book. Consider your own skill level and the instructions and safety precautions associated with the various tools and materials shown. Neither the publisher nor Black & Decker® can assume responsibility for any damage to property, injury to persons or losses incurred as a result of misuse of the information provided.

High Rectangular Deck

Simplicity, security and convenience are the hallmarks of this elevated deck.

This simple rectangular deck provides a secure, convenient, outdoor living space. The absence of a stairway prevents children from wandering away or unexpected visitors from wandering in. It also makes the deck easier to build.

Imagine how handy it will be to have this additional living area only a step away from your dining room or living room, with no more need to walk downstairs for outdoor entertaining, dining or relaxing.

And if you'd like to add a stairway, just refer to the helpful instructions in the final chapter of this book.

Cutaway View

OVERALL SIZE:
18'-0" LONG
14'-0" WIDE
9'-2" HIGH

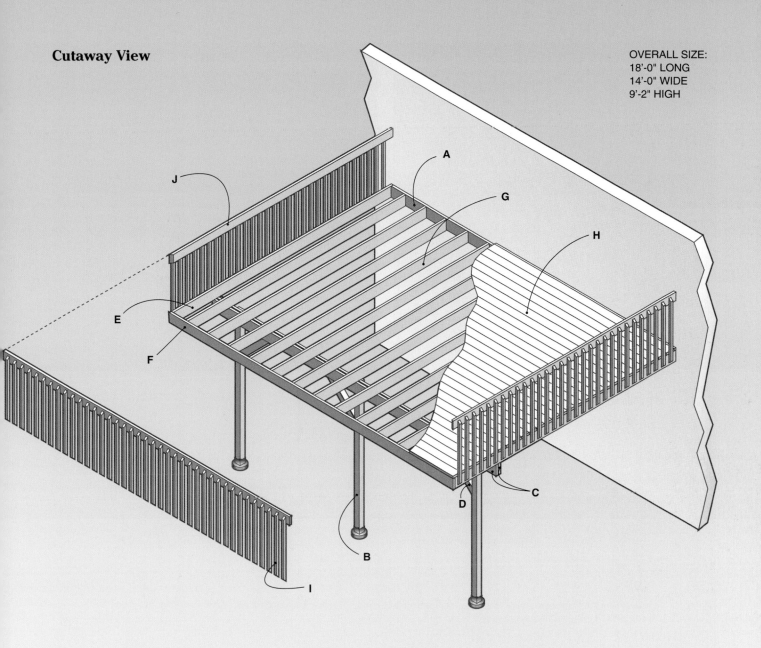

Lumber List			
Qty.	Size	Material	Part
2	2 × 12" × 20'	Trtd. lumber	Beam boards (C)
2	2 × 10" × 18'	Trtd. lumber	Ledger (A), Rim joist (F)
15	2 × 10" × 14'	Trtd. lumber	Joists (G), End joists (E)
3	6 × 6" × 10'	Trtd. lumber	Deck posts (B)
2	4 × 4" × 8'	Trtd. lumber	Braces (D)

Lumber List			
Qty.	Size	Material	Part
32	2 × 6" × 18'	Cedar	Decking (H), Top rail (J)
2	2 × 6" × 16'	Cedar	Top rail (J)
50	2 × 2" × 8'	Cedar	Balusters (I)

Supplies: 12"-diameter footing forms (3); J-bolts (3); 6 × 6" metal post anchors (3); 2 × 10" joist hangers (26); galvanized deck screws (3", 2½" and 1¼"); joist hanger nails; ⅜ × 4" lag screws and washers (28); ¼ × 5" lag screws and washers (16); ⁵⁄₁₆ × 7" carriage bolts, washers, and nuts (6); 16d galvanized nails; metal flashing (18 ft.); silicone caulk (3 tubes); concrete as required.

Framing Plan

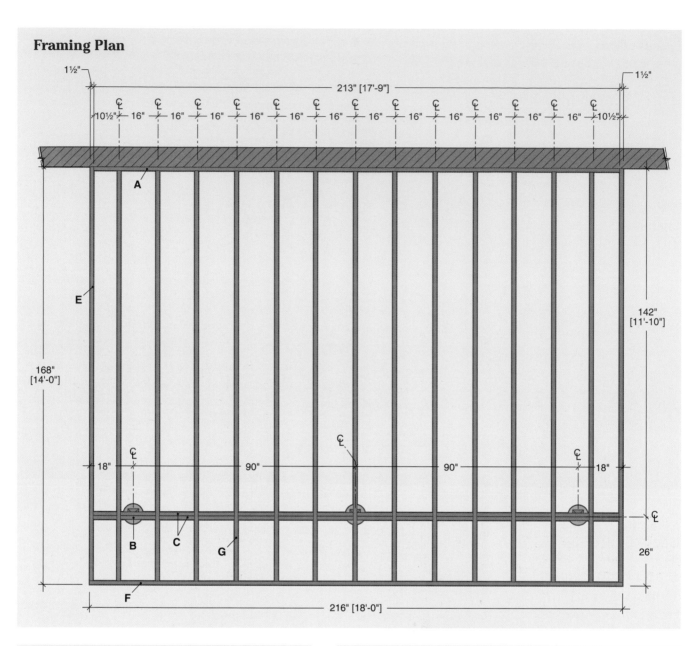

Railing Detail

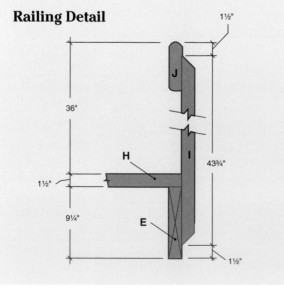

Face Board Detail

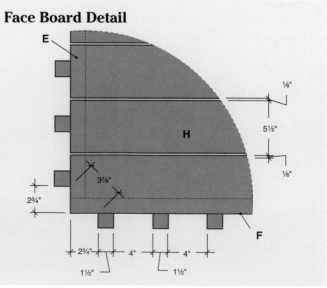

Elevation

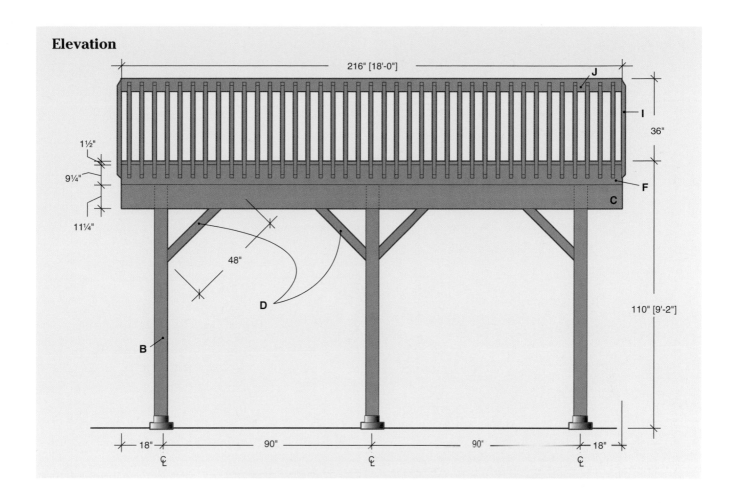

216" [18'-0"]

1½"
9¼"
11¼"
48"
36"
110" [9'-2"]
18"
90"
90"
18"

J
I
F
C
D
B

Directions:
High Rectangular Deck

ATTACH THE LEDGER.
1. Draw a level outline on the siding to show where the ledger and the end joists will fit against the house. Install the ledger so that the surface of the decking boards will be 1" below the indoor floor level **(photo A)**. This height difference prevents rainwater or melted snow from seeping into the house.
2. Cut out the siding along the outline with a circular saw. To avoid cutting the sheathing that lies underneath the siding, set the blade depth to the same thickness as the siding. Finish the cutout with a chisel, holding the beveled side in to ensure a straight cut.

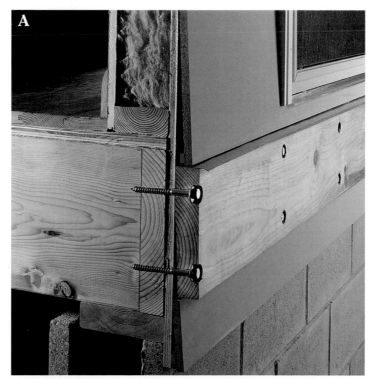

A

The ledger is anchored through the sheathing to the rim joist of the house with ⅜ × 4" lag screws. Metal flashing protects against water seepage.

To make measurements easier, drop a plumb bob from the ledger to ground level and use the 3-4-5 triangle method to check for square.

Use a template made from 2 × 4s to locate the post footings on the ground, then mark the footings with stakes.

3. Cut galvanized flashing to the length of the cutout, using metal snips. Slide the flashing up under the siding at the top of the cutout.

4. Measure and cut the ledger (A) from pressure-treated lumber. Center the ledger end to end in the cutout, with space at each end for the end joist.

5. Brace the ledger into position under the flashing. Tack the ledger into place with galvanized nails.

6. Drill pairs of ¼" pilot holes at 16" intervals through the ledger and into the house header joist. Counterbore each pilot hole ½", using a 1" spade bit. Attach the ledger with 4" lag screws and washers, using a ratchet wrench.

7. Apply silicone caulk between the siding and flashing. Also seal the lag screw heads and the cracks at the ends of the ledger.

POUR THE FOOTINGS.

1. To establish a reference point for locating the footings, drop a plumb bob from the ends of the ledger down to the ground.

2. Position a straight 14'-long 2 × 4 perpendicular to the house at the point where the plumb bob meets the ground. NOTE: If you are building on a steep slope or very uneven ground, the mason's string method of locating footing positions will work better. Refer to one of the other chapters in

this book for instructions.

3. Check for square, using the 3-4-5 triangle method. From the 2 × 4, measure 3' along the wall and make a mark. Next, measure 4' out from the house and make a mark on the 2 × 4. The diagonal line between the marks will measure 5' **(photo B)** when the board is accurately square to the house. Adjust the board as needed, and use stakes to hold it in place.

4. Extend another reference board from the house at the other end of the ledger, following the same procedure.

5. Measure out along both boards, and mark the centerline of the footings (see *Framing Plan*, page 12).

D

E

Insert the footing form into the hole, leaving 2" above the ground. Level the top, and pack soil around the form to hold it in place.

Insert a J-bolt into wet concrete at the center of the footing.

6. Lay a straight 2 × 4 between the centerline marks, and drive stakes to mark the footing locations **(photo C)**.

7. Remove the boards and dig the post footings, using a clamshell digger or power auger. Pour 2" to 3" of loose gravel into each hole for drainage. NOTE: When measuring the footing size and depth, make sure you comply with local Building Codes, which may require flaring the base to 18".

8. Cut the footing forms to length, using a reciprocating saw or handsaw, and insert them into the footing holes, leaving 2" above ground level **(photo D)**. Pack soil around the forms for support, and fill the forms with concrete, tamping with a long stick or rod to eliminate any air gaps.

9. Screed the tops flush with a straight 2 × 4. Insert a J-bolt into the center of each footing **(photo E)** and set with ¾" to 1" of thread exposed. Clean the bolt threads before the concrete sets.

SET THE POSTS.

1. Lay a long, straight 2 × 4 flat across the footings, parallel to the house. With one edge tight against the J-bolts, draw a reference line across the top of each footing to help orient the post anchors.

2. Place a metal post anchor on each footing, centering it over the J-bolt and squaring it with the reference line. Attach the post anchors by threading a nut over each bolt and tightening with a ratchet wrench.

3. The tops of the posts (B) will eventually be level with the bottom edge of the ledger, but initially cut the posts several inches longer to allow for final trimming. Position the posts in the anchors and tack into place with one nail each.

4. With a level as a guide, use braces and stakes to ensure that the posts are plumb **(photo F)**. Finish nailing the posts to the anchors.

5. Determine the height of the beam by using a chalk line and a line level. Extend the chalk line out from the bottom edge of the ledger, make

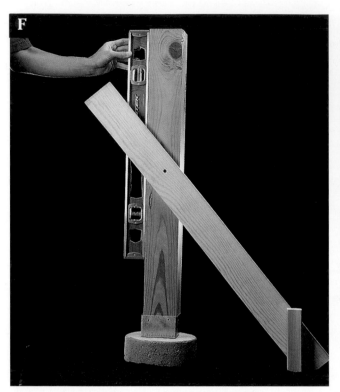

Plumb each post with a level, then use braces and stakes to hold in place until the beam and joists are installed.

Fasten the beam to the posts with carriage bolts fitted with a washer and nut. Tighten with a ratchet wrench.

sure that the line is level and snap a mark across the face of a post. Use the line and level to transfer the mark to the remaining posts.

NOTCH THE POSTS.
1. Remove the posts from the post anchors and cut to the finished height.
2. Measure and mark a 3" × 11¼" notch at the top of each post, on the outside face. Use a framing square to trace lines on all sides. Rough-cut the notches with a circular saw, then finish with a reciprocating saw or handsaw.
3. Reattach the posts to the post anchors, with the notch-side facing away from the deck.

INSTALL THE BEAM.
Installing boards of this size and length, at this height,

requires care. You should have at least two helpers.
1. Cut the beam boards (C) to length, adding several inches to each end for final trimming after the deck frame is squared up.
2. Join the beam boards together with 2½" galvanized deck screws. Mark the post locations on the top edges and sides, using a combination square as a guide.
3. Lift the beam, one end at a time, into the notches with the crown up. Align and clamp the beam to the posts.
4. Counterbore two ½"-deep holes using a 1" spade bit, then drill ⁵⁄₁₆" pilot holes through the beam and post.
5. Thread a carriage bolt into each pilot hole. Add a washer and nut to the counterbore-side of each bolt and tighten

with a ratchet wrench **(photo G)**. Seal both ends of the bolts with silicone caulk.
6. Cut tops of posts flush with top edge of beam, using a reciprocating saw or handsaw.

INSTALL THE FRAME.
1. Measure and cut the end joists (E) to length, using a circular saw.
2. Attach the end joists to the ends of the ledger with 16d galvanized nails.
3. Measure and cut the rim joist (F) to length with a circular saw. Fasten to the ends of end joists with 16d nails.
4. Square up the frame by measuring corner to corner and adjusting until the measurements are equal. When the frame is square, toenail the end joists in place on top of the beam.

5. Trim the ends of the beam flush with the faces of the end joists, using a reciprocating saw or a handsaw.

INSTALL THE BRACES.
1. Cut the braces (D) to length (see *Elevation*, page 13) with a circular saw or power miter box. Miter both ends at 45°.
2. Install the braces by positioning them against the beam boards and against the posts. Make sure the outside faces of the braces are flush with the outside faces of the beam and the posts. Temporarily fasten with deck screws.
3. Secure the braces to the

posts with 5" lag screws. Drill two ¼" pilot holes through the upper end of each brace into the beam. Counterbore to a ½"-depth using a 1" spade bit, and drive lag screws with a ratchet wrench. Repeat for the lower end of the braces into the posts.

INSTALL THE JOISTS.
1. Measure and mark the joist locations (see *Framing Plan*, page 12) on the ledger, rim joist and beam. Draw the outline of each joist on the ledger and rim joist, using a combination square.
2. Install a joist hanger at

each joist location. Attach one flange of the hanger to one side of the outline, using joist nails. Use a spacer cut from scrap 2 × 8 lumber to achieve the correct spread for each hanger, then fasten the remaining side flange with joist nails. Remove the spacer and repeat the same procedure for the remaining joist hangers.
3. Measure, mark and cut lumber for joists (G), using a circular saw. Place joists in hangers with crown side up and attach with joist hanger nails **(photo H).** Align joists with the outlines on the top of the beam, and toenail in place.

Fasten the joists in the joist hangers with 1¼" joist hanger nails. Drive nails into both sides of each joist.

Snap a chalk line flush with the outside edge of the deck, and cut off overhanging deck boards with a circular saw.

After cutting balusters to length, gang them up and drill ⅛" pilot holes through the top and bottom.

LAY THE DECKING.

1. Measure, mark and cut the decking boards (H) to length as needed.

2. Position the first row of decking flush against the house, and attach by driving a pair of galvanized deck screws into each joist.

3. Position the remaining decking boards, leaving a ⅛" gap between boards to provide for drainage, and attach to each joist with deck screws.

4. Every few rows of decking, measure from the edge of the decking to the outside edge of the deck. If the measurement can be divided evenly by 5⅝", the last board will fit flush with the outside edge of the deck as intended. If the measurement shows that the last board will not fit flush, adjust the spacing as you install the remaining rows of boards.

5. If your decking overhangs the end joists, snap a chalk line to mark the outside edge of the deck and cut flush with a circular saw set to a 1½" depth **(photo I).** If needed, finish the cut with a jig saw or handsaw where a circular saw can't reach.

BUILD THE RAILING.

1. Measure, mark and cut the balusters (I) to length, with 45° miters at both ends.

2. Gang the balusters together and drill two ⅛" pilot holes at both ends **(photo J).**

3. Clamp a 1½" guide strip flush with the bottom edge of the deck platform to establish the baluster height (see *Railing Detail*, page 12).

4. To ensure that the balusters are installed at equal intervals, create a spacing jig, less than 4" wide, from two pieces of scrap material.

5. Attach the corner balusters first (see *Face Board Detail*, page 12), using a level to ensure that they are plumb. Then use the spacing jig for positioning, and attach the remaining balusters to the deck

Rest the balusters on a 1 × 2 guide strip, and use a spacing jig to position them at equal intervals. Attach them with 3" deck screws.

platform with 3" deck screws **(photo K).**

6. Measure, mark and cut the top rail sections (J) to length. Round over three of the edges (see *Railing Detail*, page 12) using a router with a ½" round-over bit. Cut 45° miters on the ends that meet at the corners.

7. Hold or clamp the top rail in position, and attach with 2½" deck screws driven through the balusters.

8. If you need to make straight joints in the top rail, cut the ends of the adjoining boards at 45°. Drill angled ⅛" pilot holes and join with deck screws **(photo L).**

To make a joint in the top rail, cut the ends at 45° and drill a pair of pilot holes. Then fasten the ends together with deck screws.

Rectangular Deck

Extend your living space and increase your home's value.

Here's a deck that's almost classic in its simplicity. Moderately sized and easy to build, this rectangular deck won't cost you an arm and a leg—in either time or money. The framing and decking plans are quite straightforward, and you can likely build the entire deck in just two or three weekends, even with limited carpentry and building experience. Within just a few weeks time you can transform your yard into a congenial gathering place for cooking, entertaining and just plain relaxing; a place where you, your family and your friends can enjoy the fresh air in convenience and comfort.

Cutaway View

OVERALL SIZE:
12"-0" LONG
10"-0" WIDE
3'-5" HIGH

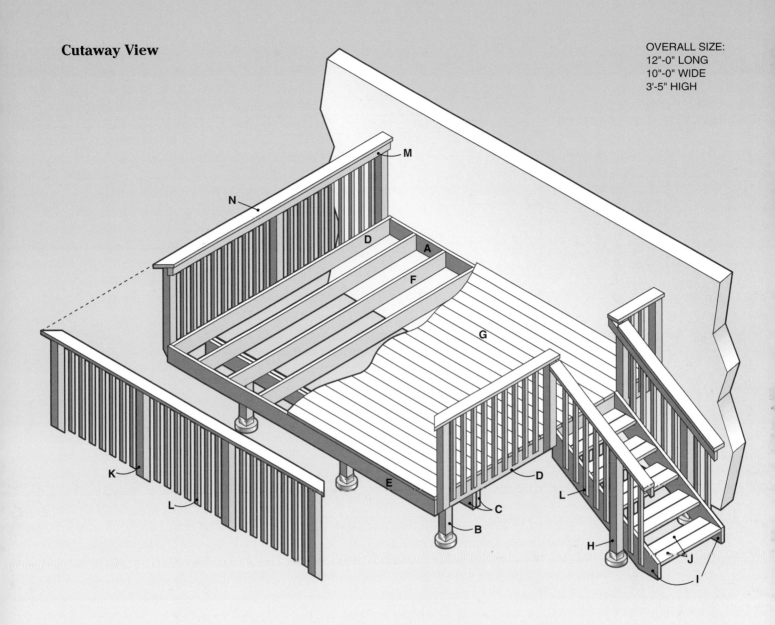

Lumber List			
Qty.	**Size**	**Material**	**Part**
4	2 × 8" × 12'	Trtd. lumber	Ledger (A), Beam bds (C), Rim joist (E)
1	4 × 4" × 8'	Trtd. lumber	Deck posts (B)
10	2 × 8" × 10'	Trtd. lumber	End joists (D), Joists (F)
25	2 × 6" × 12'	Cedar	Decking (G), Rail cap (N)
7	4 × 4" × 8'	Cedar	Stair posts (H), Rail post (K)

Lumber List			
Qty.	**Size**	**Material**	**Part**
2	2 × 12" × 8'	Cedar	Stringers (I)
5	2 × 6" × 6'	Cedar	Treads (J)
32	2 × 2" × 8'	Cedar	Balusters (L)
2	2 × 4" × 12'	Cedar	Top rail (M)
2	2 × 4" × 10'	Cedar	Top rail (M)

Supplies: 8"-diameter footing forms (5); J-bolts (5); 4 × 4" metal post anchors (5); 4 × 4" metal post-beam caps (3); 2 × 8" joist hangers (16); 1½ × 6" angle brackets (6); 1½ × 10" angle brackets (10); 3" galvanized deck screws; 16d galvanized nails; 2½" galvanized deck screws; 2½" galvanized screws; ⅜ × 4" lag screws and washers (20); ⅜ × 5" lag screws and washers (22); ¼ × 1¼" lag screws and washers (80); flashing (12 ft.); exterior silicone caulk (3 tubes); concrete as needed.

Framing Plan

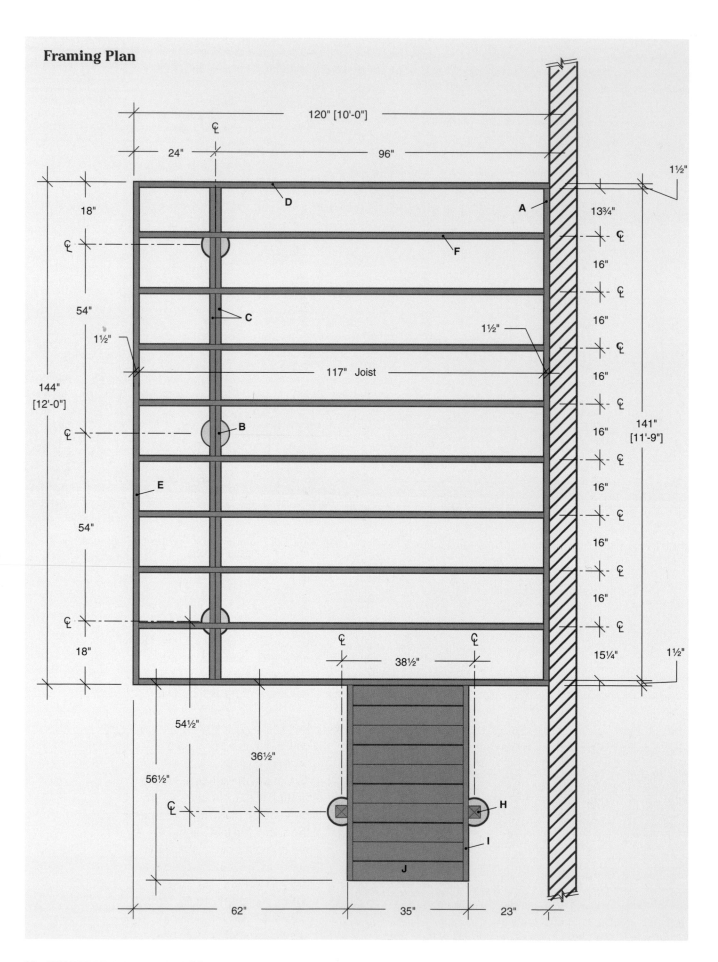

120" [10'-0"]
24"
96"
18"
13¾"
D
A
16"
16"
F
16"
54"
C
16"
1½"
1½"
117" Joist
16"
144"
[12'-0"]
16"
B
141"
[11'-9"]
16"
E
16"
54"
16"
16"
18"
15¼"
1½"
38½"
54½"
36½"
56½"
H
I
62"
35"
23"
J

Elevation

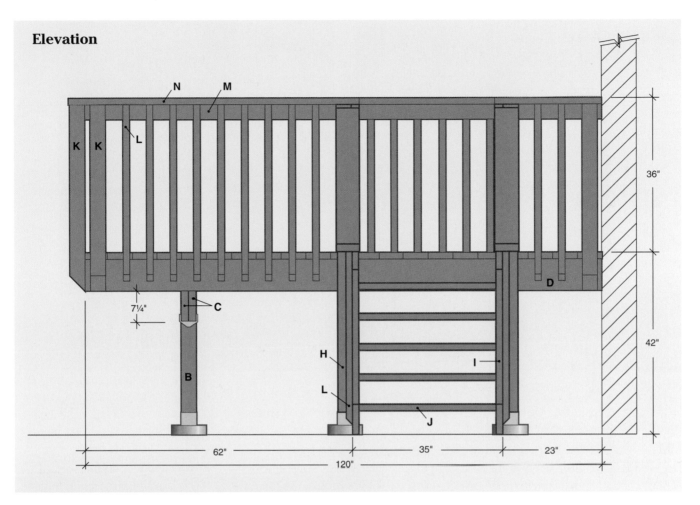

N M

K K L

36"

42"

7¼" C

B

H

L

J

D

I

62"

35"

23"

120"

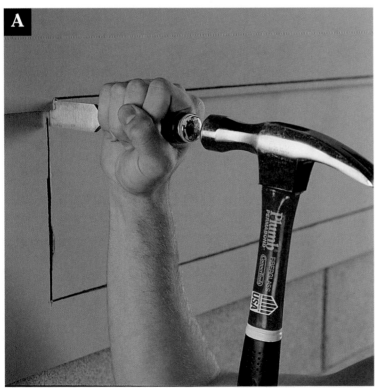

A

After outlining the position of the ledger and cutting the siding with a circular saw, use a chisel to finish the corners of the cutout.

Directions: Rectangular Deck

ATTACH THE LEDGER.

1. Draw a level outline on the siding to show where the ledger and the end joists will fit against the house. Install the ledger so that the surface of the decking boards will be 1" below the indoor floor level. This height difference prevents rainwater or melted snow from seeping into the house.

2. Cut out the siding along the outline with a circular saw. To prevent the blade from cutting the sheathing that lies underneath the siding, set the blade depth to the same thickness as the siding. Finish the cutout with a chisel **(photo A),** holding the beveled side in to ensure a straight cut.

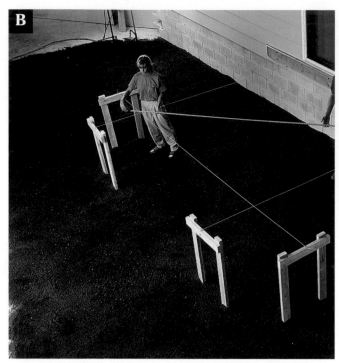

Check the strings for square, by measuring from corner to corner. If the measurements are not equal, adjust the strings on the batterboards. When the diagonal measurements are equal, the outline is square.

Drop a plumb bob from the centerpoint of each footing to transfer the location to the ground. Mark the footing locations with stakes.

3. Cut galvanized flashing to the length of the cutout, using metal snips. Slide the flashing up under the siding at the top of the cutout.

4. Measure and cut the ledger (A) from pressure-treated lumber. Center the ledger end to end in the cutout, with space at each end for the end joist.

5. Brace the ledger into position under the flashing. Tack the ledger into place with galvanized nails.

6. Drill pairs of ¼" pilot holes at 16" intervals through the ledger and into the house header joist. Counterbore each pilot hole ½", using a 1" spade bit. Attach the ledger to the wall with ⅜ × 4" lag screws and washers, using a ratchet wrench.

7. Apply a thick bead of silicone caulk between siding and flashing. Also seal the lag screw heads and the cracks at the ends of the ledger.

POUR THE FOOTINGS.

1. Referring to the measurements shown in the *Framing Plan*, page 22, mark the centerlines of the two outer footings on the ledger and drive nails at these locations.

2. Set up temporary batterboards and stretch a mason's string out from the ledger at each location. Make sure the strings are perpendicular to the ledger, and measure along the strings to find the centerpoints of the posts.

3. Set up additional batterboards and stretch another string parallel to the ledger across the post centerpoints.

4. Check the mason's strings for square **(photo B),** by measuring diagonally from corner to corner and adjusting the strings so that the measurements are equal.

5. Measure along the cross string and mark the center post

location with a piece of tape.

6. Use a plumb bob to transfer the footing centerpoints to the ground, and drive a stake to mark each point **(photo C).**

7. Remove the mason's strings and dig the post footings, using a clamshell digger or power auger. Pour 2" to 3" of loose gravel into each hole for drainage. NOTE: When measuring the footing size and depth, make sure you comply with your local Building Code, which may require flaring the base to 12".

8. Cut the footing forms to length, using a reciprocating saw or handsaw, and insert them into the footing holes, leaving 2" above ground level. Pack soil around the forms for support, and fill the forms with concrete, tamping with a long stick or rod to eliminate any air pockets.

9. Screed the tops flush with a

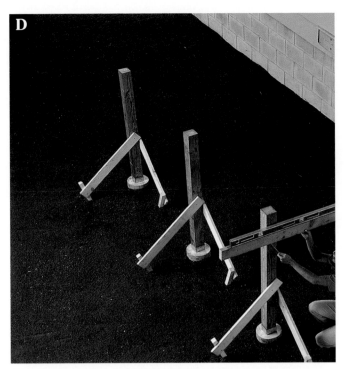

After the posts have been set in place and braced plumb, use a straight 2 × 4 and a level to mark the top of the beam on each post.

With the beam in place, align the reference marks with the post-beam caps, drill pilot holes, and fasten using 1¼" galvanized deck screws.

straight 2 × 4. Insert a J-bolt into each footing and set so ¾" to 1" of thread is exposed. Retie the mason's strings and position the J-bolts at the exact center of the posts, using a plumb bob as a guide. Clean the bolt threads before concrete sets.

SET THE POSTS.

1. Lay a long, straight 2 × 4 flat across the footings, parallel to the ledger. With one edge tight against the J-bolts, draw a reference line across each footing.
2. Place a metal post anchor on each footing, centering it over the J-bolt and squaring it with the reference line. Attach the post anchors by threading a nut over each bolt and tightening with a ratchet wrench.
3. Cut the posts to length, adding approximately 6" for final trimming. Place the posts in the anchors and tack into place with one nail.

4. With a level as a guide, use braces and stakes to plumb the posts. Finish nailing the posts to the anchors.
5. Determine the height of the beam by extending a straight 2 × 4 from the bottom edge of the ledger across the face of a post. Level the 2 × 4, and draw a line on the post **(photo D)**.
6. From that line, measure 7¼" down the post and mark the bottom of the beam. Using a level, transfer this line to the remaining posts.
7. Use a combination square to extend the level line completely around each post. Cut the posts to this finished height, using a reciprocating saw or hand saw.

INSTALL THE BEAM.

1. Cut the beam boards (C) several inches long, to allow for final trimming.
2. Join the beam boards

together with 2½" galvanized deck screws. Mark the post locations on the top edges and sides, using a combination square as a guide.
3. Attach the post-beam caps to the tops of the posts. Position the caps on the post tops, drill pilot holes, and attach using 1¼" galvanized deck screws.
4. Lift the beam into the post-beam caps, with the crown up. Align the post reference lines on the beam with the post-beam caps. NOTE: You should have at least two helpers when installing boards of this size and length, at this height.
5. Fasten the post-beam caps to the beam on both sides by drilling pilot holes, then using 1¼" deck screws to attach **(photo E)**.

INSTALL THE FRAME.

1. Measure and cut the end joists (D) to length, using a circular saw.

Cut the rim joist to length, and attach to the ends of end joists with 16d galvanized nails.

2. Attach the end joists to the ends of the ledger with 16d galvanized nails.

3. Measure and cut the rim joist (E) to length with a circular saw. Fasten to end joists with 16d nails **(photo F).**

4. Square up the frame by measuring corner to corner and adjusting until measurements are equal. Toenail the end joists in place on top of the beam, and trim the beam to length.

5. Reinforce each inside corner of the frame with an angle bracket fastened with 1¼" joist hanger nails.

INSTALL THE JOISTS.

1. Mark the outlines of the inner joists (F) on the ledger, beam and rim joist (see *Framing Plan*, page 22) using a tape measure and a combination square.

2. Attach joist hangers to the ledger and rim joist with 1¼" joist hanger nails, using a scrap 2 × 8 as a spacer to achieve the correct spread for each hanger.

3. Measure, mark and cut lumber for inner joists, using a circular saw. Place the joists in the hangers with crown side up **(photo G),** and attach at both ends with 1¼" joist hanger nails. Be sure to use all the nail holes in the hangers.

4. Align the joists with the marks on top of the beam, and toenail in place.

LAY THE DECKING.

1. Cut the first decking board (G) to length, position it against the house, and attach by driving a pair of 2½" galvanized deck screws into each joist.

2. Position the remaining decking boards with the ends overhanging the end joists. Leave a ⅛" gap between boards to provide for drainage, and attach the boards to each joist with a pair of deck screws.

3. Every few rows of decking,

measure from the edge of the decking to the outside edge of the deck. If the measurement can be divided evenly by 5⅝, the last board will fit flush with the outside edge of the deck as intended. If the measurement shows that the last board will not fit flush, adjust the spacing as you install the remaining rows of boards.

4. If your decking overhangs the end joists, snap a chalk line to mark the outside edge of the deck and cut flush with a circular saw. If needed, finish the cut with a jig saw or handsaw where a circular saw can't reach.

BUILD THE STAIRWAY.

1. Refer to the *Framing Plan*, page 22, for the position of the stairway footings.

2. Locate the footings by extending a 2 × 4 from the deck, dropping a plumb bob **(photo H)**, and marking the centerpoints with stakes.

3. Dig post holes with a

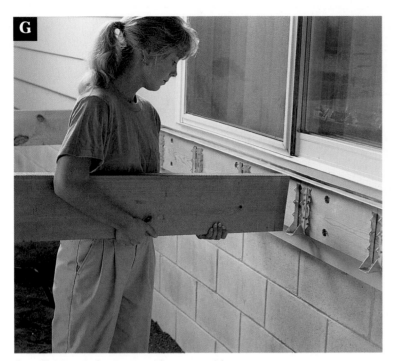

Install joists in hangers with crown side up.

clamshell digger or an auger, and pour the stairway footings using the same method as for the deck footings.

4. Attach metal post anchors to the footings, and install posts (H), leaving them long for final trimming.

5. Cut the stair stringers (I) to length and use a framing square to mark the rise and run for each step (see *Stairway Detail*, page 28). Draw the tread outline on each run. Cut the angles at the end of the stringers with a circular saw. (If you'd like more information on building stairways, see the Appendix at the back of this book.)

6. Position a 1½ × 10" angle bracket flush with the bottom of each tread line. Attach the brackets with 1¼" lag screws.

7. Fasten angle brackets to the upper ends of the stringers using 1¼" lag screws, keeping the brackets flush with cut ends on stringers. Position the top ends of the stingers on the side of

the deck, making sure the top point of the stringer and the surface of the deck are flush.

8. Attach the stringers by nailing 1¼" joist hanger nails through the angle brackets into the end joist, and by drilling ¼" pilot holes from inside the rim joist into the stringers and fastening with ⅜ × 4" lag screws.

9. To connect the stringers to the stair posts, drill two ¼" pilot holes **(photo I)** and counterbore the pilot holes ½" deep with a 1" spade bit. Use a ratchet wrench to fasten the stringers to the posts with 4" lag screws and washers.

10. Measure the length of the stair treads (J) and cut two 2 × 6 boards for each tread. For each tread, position the front board on the angle bracket so the front edge is flush with the tread outline on the stringers. Attach the tread to the brackets with ¼ × 1¼" lag screws.

11. Place the rear 2 × 6 on each tread bracket, keeping a ⅛" space between the boards.

Attach with 1¼" lag screws.
12. Attach the treads for the lowest step by driving deck screws through the stringers.

INSTALL THE RAILING.

1. Cut posts (K) and balusters (L) to length (see *Railing Detail*, page 29) with a power miter saw or circular saw. Cut the top ends square, and the bottom ends at a 45° angle.
2. Mark and drill two ¼" pilot holes at the bottom end of each post. Holes should be spaced 4" apart and counterbored ½" with a 1" spade bit.
3. Drill two ⅛" pilot holes, 4" apart, near the bottom of each baluster. At the top of each baluster, drill a pair of ⅛" pilot holes spaced 1½" apart.
4. Using a combination square, mark the locations of the posts on the outside of the deck. NOTE: Position corner posts so there is no more than

To locate the stairway footings, refer to the measurements in the Framing Plan, and extend a straight 2 x 4 perpendicularly from the deck. Use a plumb bob to transfer centerpoints to the ground.

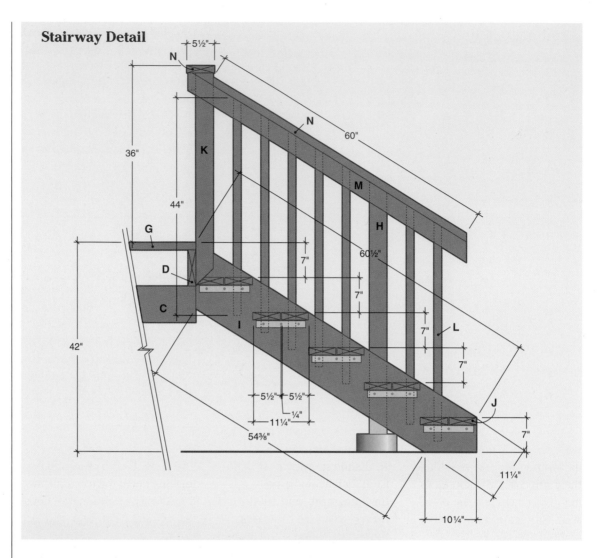

Stairway Detail

5½"

N

36"

44"

K

N   60"

M

H

G

D

60½"

C

7"

I

7"

42"

7"   L

7"

J

5½" 5½"

¼"

11¼"

54⅜"

7"

10¼"

11¼"

I

After attaching the stringers to the deck, fasten them to the posts. Drill two counterbored pilot holes through the stringers into the posts, and attach with lag screws.

4" clearance between them.
5. Clamp each post in place. Keep the beveled end flush with the bottom of the deck, and make sure the post is plumb. Use an awl to mark pilot hole locations on the side of the deck. Remove posts and drill ¼" pilot holes at marks. Attach railing posts to side of deck with ⅜ × 5" lag screws and washers.
6. Cut top rails (M) to length, with 45° miters on the ends that meet at the corners. Attach to posts with 2½" deck screws, keeping the top edge of the rail flush with the top of the posts. Join rails by cutting 45° bevels at ends.
7. Temporarily attach stair-

Railing Detail

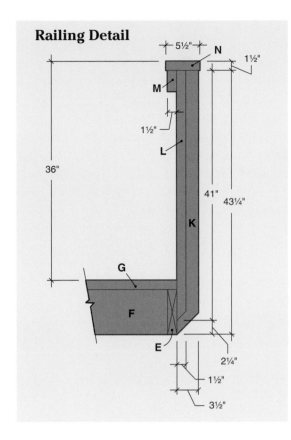

Position the stairway top rail in place against the posts. Attach temporarily and mark for cutting to size.

way top rails **(photo J)** with 3" galvanized deck screws. Mark the outline of the deck railing post and top rail on the back side of the stairway top rail. Mark the position of the top rail on the stairway post. Use a level to mark a plumb cutoff line at the lower end of the rail.

Position the rail cap over the posts and balusters. Make sure mitered corners are tight, and attach with deck screws.

Remove the rail.

8. Cut the stairway post to finished height along the diagonal mark, and cut the stairway rail along outlines. Reposition the stairway rail and attach with deck screws.

9. Attach the balusters between the railing posts at equal intervals

of 4" or less. Use deck screws, and keep the top ends of balusters flush with the top rail. On the stairway, position the balusters against the stringer and top rail, and check for plumb. Draw a diagonal cut line at top of baluster and trim to final height with a power miter saw.

10. Confirm measurements, and cut rail cap sections (N) to length. Position sections so that the inside edge overhangs the inside edge of the rail by ¼". Attach cap to rail with deck screws. At corners, miter the ends 45° and attach caps to posts **(photo K)**.

11. Cut the cap for stairway rail to length. Mark angle of deck railing post on side of cap and bevel-cut the ends of the cap. Attach cap to top rail and post with deck screws. NOTE: Local Building Codes may require a grippable handrail for any stairway over four treads. Check with your building inspector.

Inside Corner Deck

A distinctive pattern gives this deck visual appeal.

With the help of a diamond decking pattern, this inside corner deck provides a focal point for recreational activities and social gatherings. At the same time, the corner location can offer intimacy, privacy, shade and a shield from the wind.

The design calls for double joists and blocking for extra strength and stability where decking boards butt together. Joists are spaced 12" on center to support diagonal decking.

It takes a little more time to cut the decking boards and match the miter cuts, but the results are spectacular and well worth the effort.

Cutaway View

OVERALL SIZE:
14'-5" LONG
13' WIDE
4'-1" HIGH

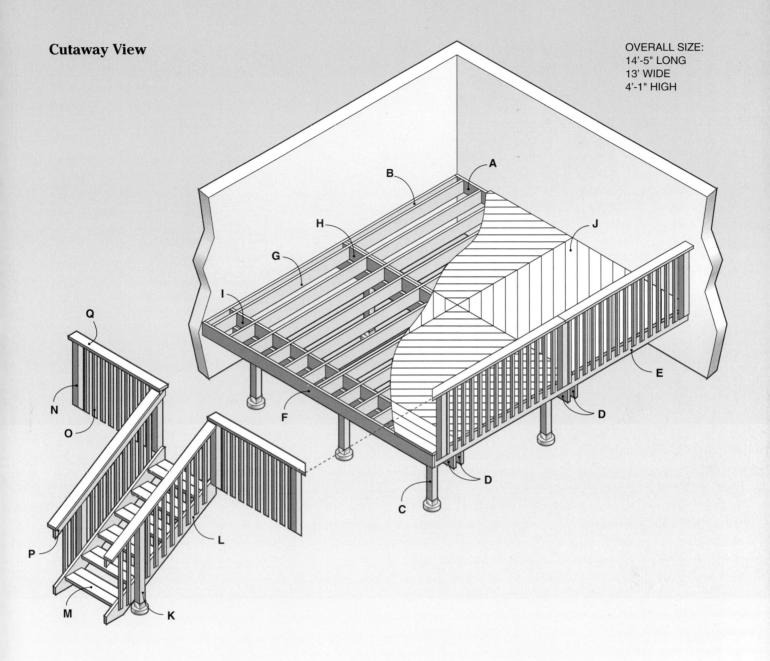

Lumber List			
Qty.	Size	Material	Part
6	2 × 8" × 14'	Trtd. lumber	Short ledger (A), Long ledger (B), Beam boards (D)
14	2 × 8" × 16'	Trtd. lumber	Joists (G), Single blocking (I)
3	2 × 8" × 8'	Trtd. lumber	Double blocking (H)
3	4 × 4" × 8'	Trtd. lumber	Deck posts (C)
1	2 × 8" × 16'	Cedar	End joist (E)
1	2 × 8" × 14'	Cedar	Rim joist (F)

Lumber List			
Qty.	Size	Material	Part
42	2 × 6" × 8'	Cedar	Decking (J), Railing caps (Q)
16	2 × 6" × 14'	Cedar	Decking (J)
1	4 × 4" × 10'	Cedar	Stair posts (K)
6	2 × 6" × 8'	Cedar	Treads (M)
4	4 × 4" × 8'	Cedar	Railing posts (N)
2	2 × 10" × 8'	Cedar	Stringers (L)
33	2 × 2" × 8'	Cedar	Balusters (O)
6	2 × 4" × 8'	Cedar	Top rails (P)

Supplies: 8"-diameter footing forms (8); J-bolts (8); 4 × 4" metal post anchors (8); 2 × 8" single joist hangers (50); 2 × 8" double joist hangers (30); 1½ × 10" angle brackets (12); 3" galvanized deck screws; 2½" galvanized deck screws; 16d galvanized nails; joist hanger nails; ⅜ × 4" lag screws and washers (78); ¼ × 1¼" lag screws (96); ½ × 7" carriage bolts, washers, and nuts (12); exterior silicone caulk (6 tubes); concrete as needed.

GREAT DECKS & FURNISHINGS   31

Framing Plan

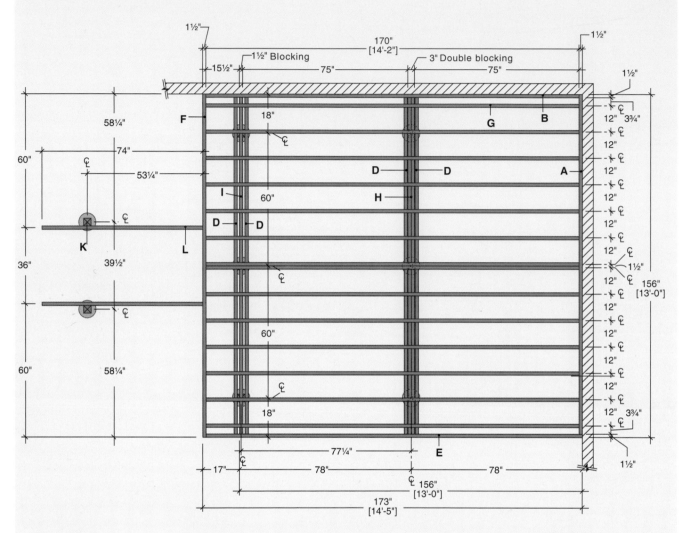

Elevation

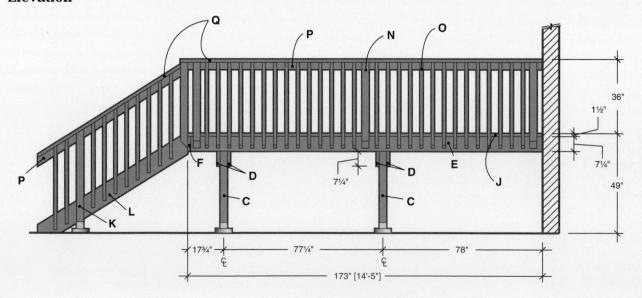

Railing Detail

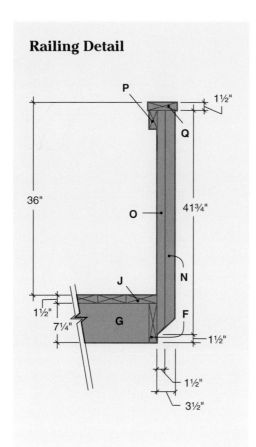

Stairway Detail

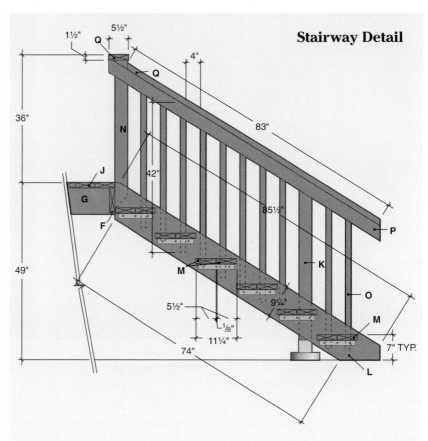

Directions:
Inside Corner Deck

ATTACH THE LEDGERS.
The inside angle of the house should form a right angle. If there is a slight deviation, use shims behind the ledger to create a 90° angle in the corner.

1. To show where the ledgers will be attached to the house, draw outlines on the wall, using a level as a guide. To locate the top of the ledger outline, measure down from the indoor floor surface 1" plus the thickness of the decking boards. This height difference prevents rain and melting snow from seeping into the house.

2. Measure and cut the ledgers to length. They will be shorter than the outline on the wall to allow for the width of the rim joist and end joist.

Once pilot holes have been drilled and the ledger has been positioned and braced against the wall, use a ratchet wrench to attach the ledger with lag screws and washers.

To locate the centerpoints of the footings on the ground, drop a plumb bob from the intersections of the mason's strings. Then, drive a stake into the ground to mark each centerpoint.

Post anchors keep the post above the footing to discourage rot. The post rests on a metal pedestal that fits over a J-bolt mounted in the footing.

3. Drill pairs of ¼" pilot holes through the ledgers at 16" intervals. Counterbore the pilot holes ½" with a 1" spade bit.

4. Brace the short ledger (A) in place, and insert a nail or an awl through the pilot holes to mark the hole locations on the wall.

5. Repeat the process to mark the hole locations for the long ledger (B).

6. Remove the ledgers and drill pilot holes into the stucco with a ⅜" masonry bit. Then, use a ¼" bit to extend each pilot hole through the sheathing and into the header joist.

7. Position and brace the ledgers against the walls. Use a ratchet wrench to attach the ledgers to the walls with ⅜ × 4" lag screws and washers **(photo A).** Seal the screw heads and all cracks between the wall and ledger with silicone caulk.

POUR THE DECK FOOTINGS. To locate the footings, stretch mason's strings between the ledgers and 2 × 4 supports, known as batterboards.

1. Referring to the measurements shown in the *Framing Plan*, page 32, mark the centerlines of the footings on the ledgers and drive a nail into the ledger at each location.

2. Set up temporary batterboards and stretch a mason's string out from the ledger at each location. Make sure the strings are perpendicular to the ledger.

3. Check the mason's strings for square, using the 3-4-5 triangle method. From the point where each string meets the ledger, measure 3' along the ledger and make a mark. Next, measure 4' out along the string and mark with tape. The distance between the points on the ledger and the string should be 5'. If it's not, adjust the string position on

the batterboard accordingly.

4. Drop a plumb bob to transfer the footing centerpoints to the ground, and drive a stake to mark each point **(photo B).** Remove the strings.

5. Dig the post footings, using a clamshell digger or power auger. Pour 2" to 3" of loose gravel into each hole for drainage. NOTE: Make sure the footing size and depth comply with your local Building Code, which may require flaring the base to 12".

6. Cut the footing forms to length, using a reciprocating saw or handsaw, and insert them into the footing holes so that they extend 2" above grade. Pack soil around the forms for support, and fill the forms with concrete, tamping with a long stick or rod to eliminate any air pockets.

7. Screed the tops of the footings flush, using a 2 × 4. Insert a J-bolt into the wet concrete of each footing, and set it, with

¾" to 1" of thread exposed. Retie the mason's strings and position each J-bolt at the exact center of the post location, using the plumb bob as a guide. Clean the bolt threads before the concrete sets.

SET THE POSTS.
1. Lay a long, straight 2 × 4 flat across each row of footings, parallel to the short ledger. With one edge tight against the J-bolts, draw a reference line across the top of each footing.
2. Center a metal post anchor over the J-bolt on each footing, and square it with the reference line. Attach the post anchors by threading a nut over each bolt and tightening with a ratchet wrench.
3. Cut the posts, leaving an

extra 6" for final trimming. Place each post in an anchor **(photo C)** and tack it in place with one nail.
4. With a level as a guide, use braces and stakes to ensure that each post is plumb. Finish nailing the posts to the anchors.
5. Determine the height of the inside beam by extending a straight 2 × 4 from the bottom edge of the long ledger across the row of posts. Level the 2 × 4, and draw a line on the posts. Use the same method to determine the height of the outer beam.

INSTALL THE BEAMS.
1. Cut the beam boards (D), leaving an extra few inches for final trimming.
2. Position one beam board,

crown up, against the row of posts. Tack the board in place with deck screws **(photo D).**
3. Attach the remaining beam boards to the posts in the same way.
4. Drill two ½" holes through the boards and posts at each joint and counterbore the pilot holes ½" with a 1" spade bit. Secure the beam boards to the posts with carriage bolts, using a ratchet wrench.
5. Cut the tops of the posts flush with the tops of the beams, using a reciprocating saw or handsaw.

INSTALL THE JOISTS.
A double joist at the center of the deck provides extra support for the ends of the decking boards.
1. Measure, mark and cut the end joist (E) and the rim joist (F), using a circular saw.
2. Attach the end joist to the short ledger and the rim joist to the long ledger, using 16d galvanized nails.
3. Nail the rim joist to the end joist **(photo E).**
4. Toenail the end joist to the tops of the beams, and cut the ends of the beams flush with the end joist.
5. Measure, mark and install the double center joist at the precise center of the deck, with double joist hangers.
6. Measure both ways from the double joist, and mark the centerpoints of the remaining joists at 12" intervals. Using a combination square, mark the outlines of the joists on the ledger, beams and rim joist.
7. Nail the joist hangers to the short ledger and rim joist, using a scrap 2 × 8 as a spacer to achieve the correct spread for each hanger.

Position the beam against the posts, and attach it temporarily with deck screws.

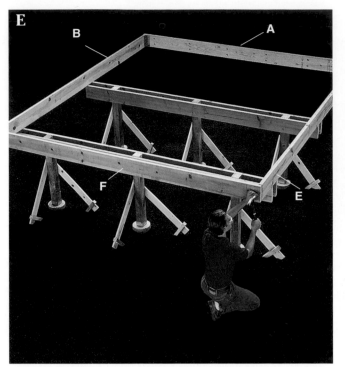

Drive 16d galvanized nails through the rim joist and into the end joist.

Working from a plywood platform, install double blocking to support the ends of the deck boards. Attach the blocking by alternating end nailing with using joist hangers.

8. Cut the joists (G) to length. Insert the joists into the hangers with the crown up, and attach them with joist hanger nails. Align the joists with the marks on the beams and toenail them in place.

INSTALL THE BLOCKING. The ends of the decking boards in the diamond pattern are supported by a row of double blocking at the center of the pattern and a row of single blocking at the edge of the pattern.

1. To locate the rows of blocking, measure from the inside corner of the house along the long ledger (see *Framing Plan*, page 32). Drive one screw or nail at 78", and another at 156". Make corresponding marks across from the ledger on the end joist.

2. Snap chalk lines across the joists, between the ledger and

the end joist. The line at 78" is the centerline of the double blocking. The line at 156" is the outer edge of the single blocking. Don't be concerned if the blocking is not directly over the beams.

3. Cut double blocking pieces from 2 × 8s nailed together with 16d galvanized nails.

4. Install the blocking by alternating end nailing or screwing with using galvanized joist hangers **(photo F).**

LAY THE DECKING. Except for the three rows of straight decking at the top of the stairway, the decking is laid in a diamond pattern.

1. Begin at the center of the diamond pattern, where the double joist and the double blocking intersect. Cut four identical triangles, as large as possible, from 2 × 6" cedar stock.

2. Drill ⅛" pilot holes in the ends, position the pieces as shown **(photo G),** and attach with 3" deck screws.

3. To install the remaining courses, measure, cut, drill, and attach the first three boards in each course. Then, measure the actual length of the last board **(photo G)** to achieve the best fit. For best results, install the decking course by course. Maintain a ⅛" gap between courses.

4. Once the diamond decking pattern is complete, cut and install the three remaining deck boards.

BUILD THE STAIRS.

1. For the position of the stairway footings, refer to the *Framing Plan* on page 32. Locate the footings by extending a 2 × 4 from the deck, perpendicular to the rim joist, dropping a plumb bob, and

G

To achieve the best fit, measure the actual length of the last deck board in each course before cutting.

marking the centerpoints on the ground with stakes.

2. Dig postholes with a clamshell digger or an auger, and pour footings using the same method as for the deck footings. Insert J-bolts, leaving ¾" to 1" of thread exposed. Allow the concrete to set. Attach metal post anchors.

3. Cut the stairway posts (K) to length, adding approximately 6" for final trimming. Place the posts in the anchors.

4. Use a level to ensure that the posts are plumb, and attach the posts to the anchors with deck screws.

5. Cut the stringers (L) to length and use a framing square to mark the rise and run for each step (see *Stairway Detail*, page 33). Draw the tread outline on each run. Cut the angles at the ends of the stringers with a circular saw. (For a more detailed de-

scription of stairway construction, see *Changing Stairway Height*, pages 102 to 103.)

6. Position an angle bracket flush with the bottom of each tread outline. Drill ⅛" pilot holes in the stringers, and attach the angle brackets with 1¼" lag screws.

7. The treads (M) fit between the stringers, and the stringers fit between the stairway posts. Measure and cut the treads (M) to length, 3" shorter than the distance between the stairway posts.

8. Assemble the stairway upside down on sawhorses. Mark and drill ⅛" pilot holes at the ends of the treads. Position each front tread with its front edge flush to the tread outline, and attach to the angle brackets with ¼ × 1¼" lag screws.

9. Attach the rear treads in similar fashion **(photo H),** leaving a ⅛" gap between treads.

10. Position the stairway in place against the edge of the deck, making sure the top of the stringer is flush with the surface of the deck. From underneath the deck, drill ¼" pilot holes through the rim joist into the stringers. Attach the stringers to the rim joist with 4" lag screws, using a ratchet wrench **(photo I).**

11. To fasten the stairway to the stair posts, drill two ¼" pilot holes through each stringer into a post. Counterbore the pilot holes ½" deep with a 1" spade bit, and use a ratchet wrench to drive 4" lag screws with washers. Seal the screw heads with silicone caulk.

INSTALL THE DECK RAILING.

1. Cut the railing posts (N) and balusters (O) to length (see *Railing Detail*, page 33) with a power miter box or circular saw. Cut the tops square and the bottoms at 45° angles.

2. Drill two ¼" pilot holes at the bottom end of each railing post, positioned so the lag screws will attach to the rim joist. Counterbore the holes ½" deep with a 1" spade bit.

3. Drill two ⅛" pilot holes near the bottom of each baluster, spaced 4" apart. At the top of each baluster, drill a pair of ⅛" pilot holes spaced 1½" apart.

TIP

When laying decking, install boards that have a flat grain with the bark side down. Flat-grain boards tend to cup to the bark side and, if installed bark-side-up, often trap water on the deck.

H

Attach the treads to the stringers using 1¼" lag screws and angle brackets.

I

Fasten the stair to the deck with a ratchet wrench using 4" lag screws.

4. With the help of a combination square, draw the outlines of the railing posts around the perimeter of the deck. The posts at the corner must be spaced so there is less than 4" between them.

5. Hold each railing post in its position, with the end 1½" above the bottom edge of the deck platform (See *Railing Detail,* page 33). Make sure the post is plumb, and insert an awl through the counterbored holes to mark pilot hole locations on the deck.

6. Set the post aside and drill ¼" pilot holes at the marks. Attach the railing posts to the deck with ⅜ × 4" lag screws and washers. Seal the screw heads with silicone caulk.

7. Cut the top rails (P) to length with the ends mitered at 45° where they meet in the corner. Attach them to the railing posts with 3" deck screws, keeping the edges of

the rails flush with the tops of the posts.

8. To position the balusters, measure the total distance between two railing posts, and mark the centerpoint on the top rail. The two railing sections on the long side of this deck will have a baluster at the centerpoint; the two railing sections on the stairway side will have a space at the centerpoint. NOTE: If the dimensions of your deck vary from the plan, calculate whether you will have a baluster or a space at the center of each section.

9. Cut a spacer slightly less than 4" wide. Start at the center of each railing section, and position either a baluster or a space over the line. Measure out from the center both ways, marking the outlines of the balusters on the top rail. The end spaces may be narrow, but they will be symmetrical.

10. To install the balusters, begin next to a railing post and make sure the first baluster is plumb. Install the remaining balusters, holding each one tight against the spacer and flush with the top rail. Attach the balusters with 2½" deck screws.

11. Cut the deck railing cap (Q) to length, with the ends mitered at 45° where they meet in the corner. Position the railing cap sections so the inside edge overhangs the inside edge of the top rail by ¼" **(photo J).** Attach the cap with 3" deck screws.

INSTALL THE
STAIRWAY RAILING.

1. Determine the exact size and shape of the stairway top rail. Tack a cedar 2 × 4 across the faces of the stairway post and deck post with 10d galvanized nails. Make sure the angle of the 2 × 4 is parallel

J

After the top rail and balusters have been installed, install the railing cap with its inside edge overhanging the inside face of the top rail by ¼".

K

With the stairway top rail cut to size and installed, attach the railing cap with deck screws.

with the angle of the stringer below.

2. On the back side of the 2 × 4 mark the outline of the deck railing post and the end of the deck top rail. On the stairway post, mark a diagonal cutoff line at the top edge of the 2 × 4. At the lower end of the 2 × 4, use a level to mark a plumb cutoff line directly above the end of the stringer.

3. Remove the 2 × 4 and make the cuts.

4. Drill ⅛" pilot holes through the stairway top rail. Place in position and attach with 2½" deck screws.

5. To trim the top ends of the stairway balusters, hold a baluster against the stairway post and draw a diagonal cut line along the top edge of the rail. Trim the baluster. Using this baluster as a template, mark and cut the remaining stairway balusters.

6. Install the stairway balusters with 2½" deck screws, using the same procedure as for the deck balusters.

7. Measure the railing caps for the stairway. Cut the caps to size, with the upper ends beveled to fit against the deck posts, and the lower ends beveled to align with the end of the top rail. Install the caps by drilling ⅛" pilot holes and attaching them with deck screws **(photo K).**

Island Deck

*The perfect place
to visit when you
need to relax.*

An island deck can transform any area of your yard into a virtual oasis. Since it's not attached to your house, you can position your island deck wherever you like—to capitalize on a spectacular view or to catch the cool afternoon breeze in a shady glen.

Accessible and inviting with its three-sided landing, this deck welcomes visitors of all ages. And it can readily serve as a cornerstone for a total landscaping plan; one that will make your entire yard a more comfortable and attractive space for enjoying the great outdoors.

Cutaway View

OVERALL SIZE:
14'-1½" LONG
14'-1½" WIDE
2'-4" HIGH

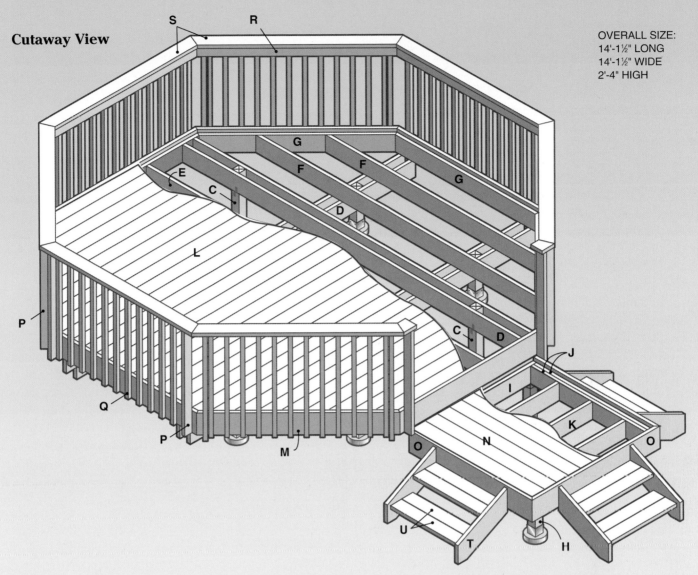

Lumber List					Lumber List			
Qty.	Size	Material	Part		Qty.	Size	Material	Part
4	2 × 4" × 16'	Pine	Site chooser sides (A)		25	2 × 6" × 14'	Cedar	Deck decking (L), Railing cap (S)
2	2 × 4" × 12'	Pine	Site chooser diagonals (B)		7	2 × 6" × 12'	Cedar	Deck decking (L)
2	4 × 4" × 12'	Trtd. lumber	Deck posts (C), Landing posts (H)		13	2 × 6" × 10'	Cedar	Deck decking (L), Landing decking (N), Treads (U)
10	2 × 8" × 14'	Trtd. lumber	Beam bds (D)		4	2 × 6" × 8'	Cedar	Deck decking (L)
			Long joists (E)		11	2 × 10" × 6'	Cedar	Deck face boards (M), Landing face boards (O)
2	2 × 8" × 12'	Trtd. lumber	Mitered joists (F)					
6	2 × 8" × 10'	Trtd. lumber	Mitered joists (F), Inner rim joists (I), Outer rim joists (J), Landing joists (K)		8	2 × 4" × 8'	Cedar	Railing posts (P)
					42	2 × 2" × 8'	Cedar	Balusters (Q)
					7	2 × 4" × 6'	Cedar	Top rail (R)
9	2 × 8" × 6'	Trtd. lumber	Deck rim joists (G), Landing joists (K)		3	2 × 10" × 6'	Cedar	Stringers (T)

Supplies: 8"-diameter footing forms (12); J-bolts (12); 4 × 4" metal post anchors (12); 90° 2 × 8" joist hangers (10); 45° 2 × 8" joist hangers (8); joist ties (16); post-beam caps (4); joist hanger nails; 1½" × 10" angle brackets (12); 3" galvanized deck screws; ¼ × 1¼" galvanized lag screws and washers (96); 16d galvanized box nails; ½ × 7" carriage bolts, washers, and nuts (16); ⅜ × 5" lag screws and washers (32); concrete as required.

Framing Plan

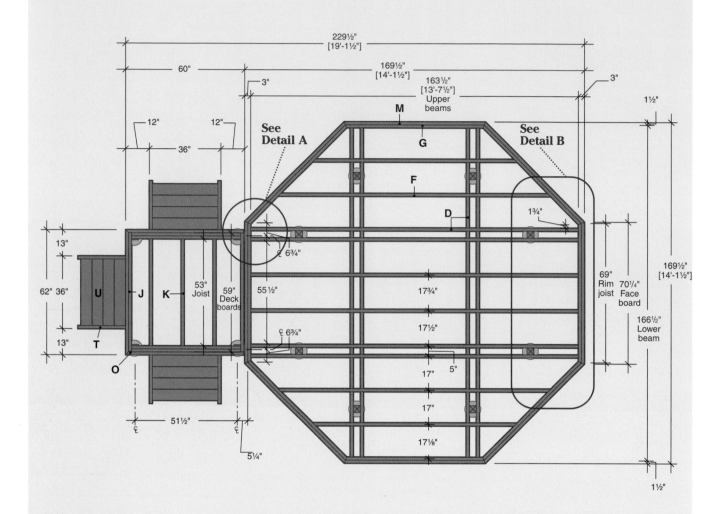

229½"
[19'-1½"]

60"

169½"
[14'-1½"]

163½"
[13'-7½"]
Upper beams

3"

3"

1½"

12"

12"

36"

See Detail A

M

See Detail B

G

F

169½"
[14'-1½"]

13"

D

1¾"

62" 36"

U

J

K

53" Joist

59" Deck boards

55½"

¢ 6¾"

17¾"

69" Rim joist

70¼" Face board

166½" Lower beam

13"

T

O

¢ 6¾"

17½"

17"

5"

51½"

17"

17"

5¼"

17⅛"

1½"

Elevation

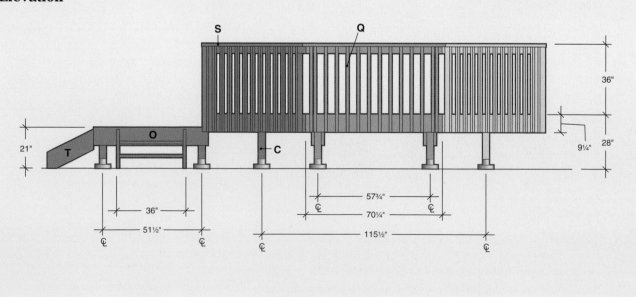

S

Q

36"

T

O

C

21"

9¼"

28"

36"

51½"

57¾"

70¼"

115½"

Detail A

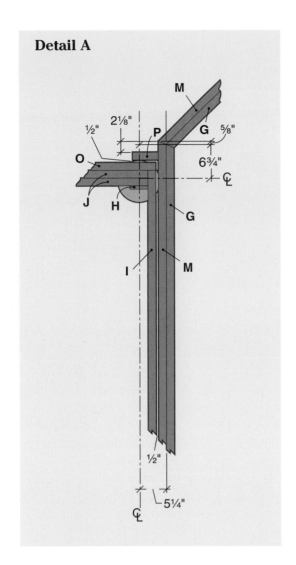

M

2⅛"
½"   P   G   ⅝"

O   6¾"
C̶L

J   H   G

I   M

½"

5¼"

C̶L

Detail B

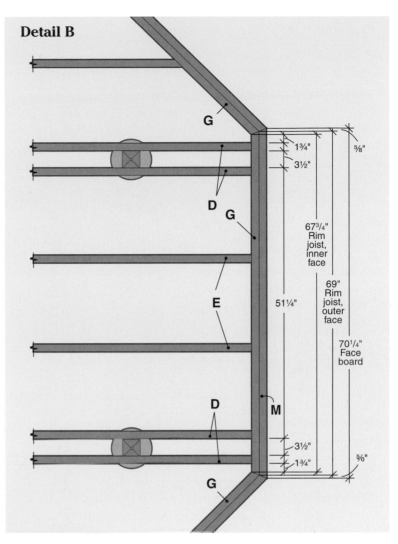

G

1¾"
3½"   ⅝"

D   G

67¾"
Rim
joist,
inner
face

69"
Rim
joist,
outer
face

E   51¼"

70¼"
Face
board

D   M

3½"
1¾"   ⅝"

G

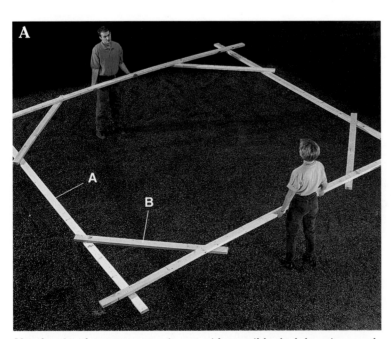

A

A

B

Use the site chooser to experiment with possible deck locations and to find the site you like best.

Directions: Island Deck

POSITION THE DECK.
1. Measure, mark and cut to length the site chooser frame (A) and diagonal braces (B) (see *Site Chooser Detail*, page 44).
2. Fasten the frame together with 3" deck screws, and check for squareness by measuring corner to corner. Adjust the frame so measurements are identical, and attach the diagonal braces with deck screws.
3. With a helper, move the site chooser to select the exact deck location **(Photo A).**
4. When you've established the deck position, set the site

Locate the deck footings by stretching mason's strings across the site chooser, marking the footing locations with tape, and dropping a plumb bob from each mark.

Insert a J-bolt, then drop a plumb bob to check for exact center of the footings.

chooser on sawhorses and tack or clamp in place to conveniently find the footing locations.

LOCATE THE FOOTINGS.
1. Mark the footing center-lines on the frame and stretch mason's strings across the site from mark to mark. Measure along the strings, marking the footing locations with tape.
2. Drop a plumb bob from each marked location, and drive stakes into the ground to mark the centers of the deck footings **(Photo B).**

POUR THE FOOTINGS.
1. Remove the mason's strings and dig the footing holes, using a clamshell dig-ger or power auger.
2. Pour 2" to 3" of loose gravel into each hole for drainage, making sure hole dimensions comply with your local Build-ing Code, which may require flaring the base to 12".
3. Cut concrete tube forms to length, using a reciprocating saw or handsaw. Insert tubes into holes, leaving 2" of tube above ground level.
4. Pack soil around tubes and fill tubes with concrete, tamp-ing with a long stick or rod to eliminate any air gaps.
5. Screed the concrete flush with a straight 2 × 4, and insert a J-bolt into each footing, leav-ing ¾" to 1" of the thread

Site Chooser Detail

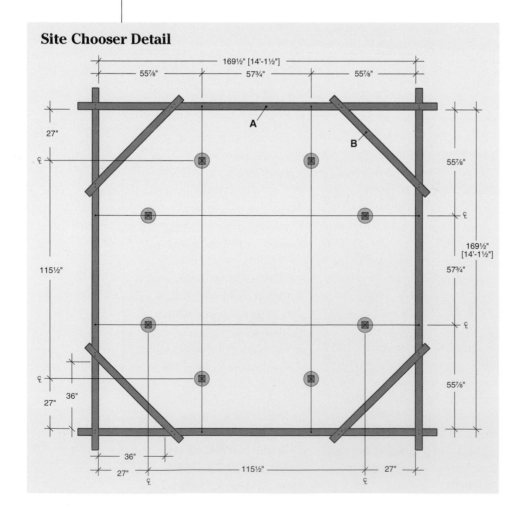

D

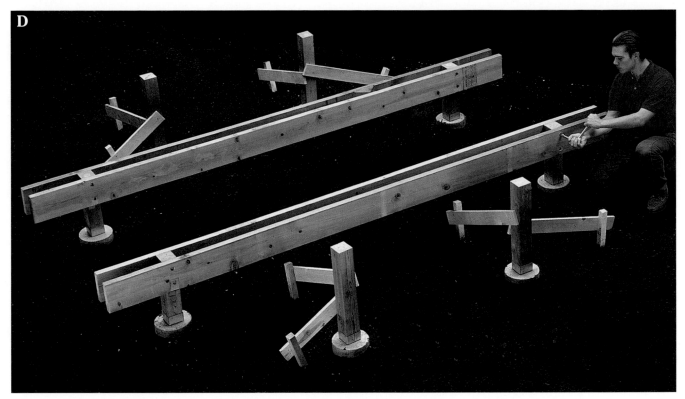

After trimming the lower posts to length, permanently attach the deck beams to the posts with carriage bolts, using a ratchet wrench. The upper deck beams will be perpendicular to, and rest on top of, the lower deck beams.

exposed. Retie the mason's strings and position the J-bolt at the center of the footing, using a plumb bob as a guide **(Photo C)**.

6. Clean bolt threads before concrete sets.

SET THE DECK POSTS.

1. Lay a straight 2 × 4 flat across each pair of footings, with one edge tight against the J-bolts. Draw a line across the top of each footing to help orient the post anchors.

2. Place a metal post anchor on each footing, centering it over the J-bolt and squaring it with the reference line. Thread a nut over each J-bolt and tighten the post anchors in place.

3. Cut the deck posts (C) several inches long to allow for final trimming. Set the posts in the anchors, brace the taller

posts plumb, and nail the posts in place.

4. Establish the height of the taller posts by measuring up 26½" from ground level and marking one post. Using a mason's string and a line level, transfer this mark to the remaining three tall posts.

5. To establish the height of the lower beam posts, measure down 7¼" from the first line and transfer a level mark to the four lower posts.

INSTALL THE DECK BEAMS. This deck uses two sets of beams. The lower beams are three inches longer than the upper beams, because the rim joists rest on them. The lower beams support the upper beams and the deck platform.

1. Measure, mark and cut the four lower beam boards (D) to length.

2. Mark the post locations on the tops and sides of the lower beams, using a combination square as a guide.

3. Position the lower beams crown-side-up on their posts. Make sure they are level, and fasten them with deck screws.

4. Trim the tops of the posts flush with a reciprocating saw or a handsaw.

5. Drill two ½" holes through the beams at each post. Securely attach the lower beams with carriage bolts and washers, using a ratchet wrench **(Photo D)**.

6. Measure, mark and cut the upper beams (D) to length. Mark post locations and attach, following the same steps as for the lower beams.

INSTALL THE RIM JOISTS.

1. Cut four of the eight rim joists (G) to length (see *Detail*

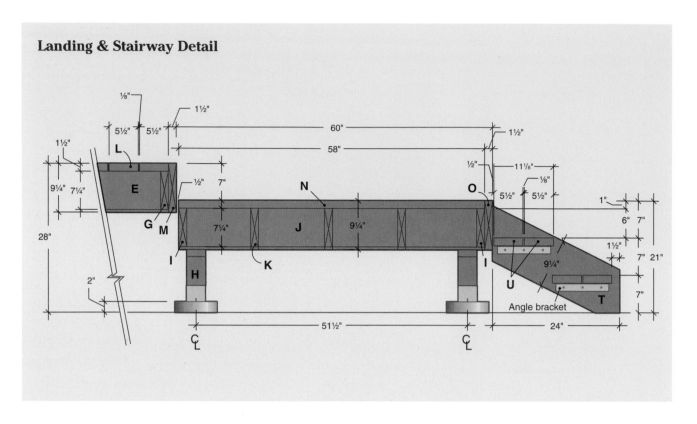

B, page 43), using a circular saw. Make 22½° miter cuts on the ends.

2. Attach one rim joist to each end of the upper beams (see *Detail B*, page 43) by nailing through the rim joist into the beams with box nails. Toenail the remaining two rim joists to the tops of the lower beams.

3. Verify the measurements of the remaining rim joists, cut to length, miter the ends at 22½°, and install. At the corners, drill pairs of ⅛" pilot holes and fasten the adjacent rim joists to each other with deck screws.

POUR LANDING FOOTINGS AND INSTALL POSTS.

1. Locate the landing footings by stretching a mason's string out from the rim joist to a batter board, according to the measurements on the *Framing Plan*, page 42, and *Detail A*, page 43. Make sure the strings are perpendicular to the rim joist and are parallel with each other.

2. Mark the footing locations with tape. Use a plumb bob and stakes to transfer the locations to the ground **(Photo E).**

3. Remove the mason's strings and dig holes for the footings, using a clamshell digger or power auger. Pour 2" to 3" of loose gravel into each hole for drainage, making sure hole dimensions comply with your local Building Code.

4. Cut concrete tube forms to length, using a reciprocating saw or handsaw. Insert tubes into holes, leaving 2" of tube above ground level. Pack soil around tubes and fill tubes with concrete, tamping the concrete to eliminate air gaps.

5. Screed the tops flush and insert a J-bolt into each footing, leaving ¾" to 1" of the thread exposed. Retie the mason's strings and position the J-bolt at the centerpoint of the footing, using a plumb bob. Clean bolt threads before concrete sets.

6. Install post anchors, cut the landing posts to length (see *Detail*, above), and attach the posts to the post anchors.

INSTALL LANDING BEAMS AND RIM JOISTS.

1. Attach post-beam caps to the tops of the landing posts.

2. Verify size, mark, and cut the beam boards (J) and rim joists (I) to length, using a circular saw (see *Framing Plan*, page 42).

3. Hold one pair of beam boards together, then measure and mark the post-beam cap locations on the tops and sides of the boards, using a combination square. Repeat for the second pair of boards.

4. Place beams, crown side up, into the post-beam caps and align. Drill pilot holes and fasten the caps to the beams with deck screws.

5. Position the rim joists flush with the side and top of the beams (see *Detail A*, page 43),

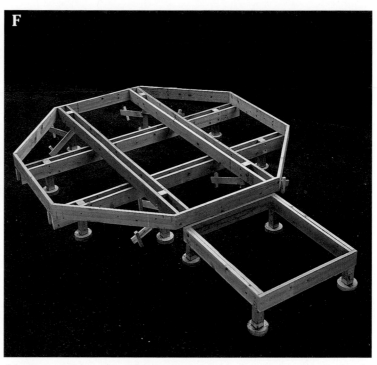

Locate the landing footings with mason's string and a plumb bob.

Measure, mark and cut the landing beams. Attach them to the landing posts, using post-beam caps.

drill ⅛" pilot holes through the rim joists, and fasten with deck screws **(Photo F).**

INSTALL DECK AND LANDING JOISTS

For the deck, the inner joists are installed with joist hangers and toenailed to the tops of the lower beams. This deck uses 90° joist hangers for the landing and for the two deck joists between the upper beams. For the angled deck joists, we used 45° joist hangers.

1. Using the plan, measure along the deck rim joists and lower beams, marking where joists are attached. Draw the outline of each joist on the rim joists and lower beams, using a combination square as a guide.

2. Measure, mark and cut lumber for long joists (E) and mitered joists (F), using a circular saw. Mark the ends of

Straighten out any bowed decking boards with a pry bar and attach, using decking screws, leaving a ⅛" gap between boards.

Railing Detail

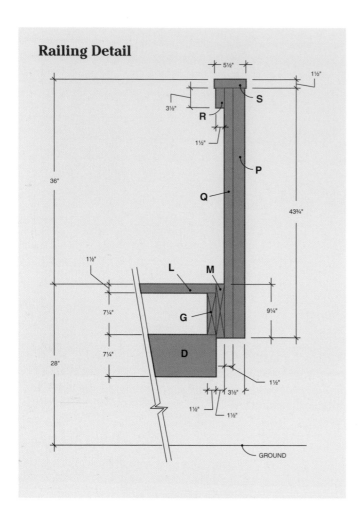

Face Board Detail

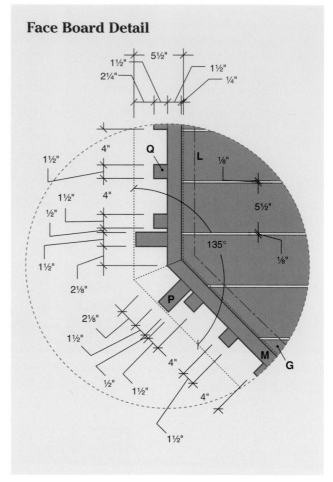

the mitered joists with a 22½°
angle, using a speed square,
and cut the ends.
3. Place joists in hangers with
crown side up, and attach
with nails. Align joists with the
outlines on the top edges of
the lower beams and toenail
in place.
4. Measure and mark locations of landing joists (K) on
landing rim joists. Position
joist hangers and attach with
nails. Install landing joists and
nail in place.

LAY THE DECK DECKING.
1. Measure, cut and position
the first row of decking (L)
next to the landing, and attach by driving a pair of deck
screws into each joist.
2. Position the remaining

decking boards so ends overhang the rim joists, leaving a
⅛" gap between the boards to
provide for drainage **(Photo
G).** Attach boards to each joist
with a pair of deck screws.
3. After installing every few
rows of decking, measure
from the edge of the decking
to the far edge of the deck.
Adjust the spacing between
the remaining boards so the final board can be full width.
4. Snap a chalk line on the
decking to mark a line flush
with the outside edge of the
deck and trim the deck
boards with a circular saw.

INSTALL THE FACE BOARDS.
1. Measure, mark and cut
deck face boards (M). Miter-
cut the ends at 22½°. Position

face boards flush with decking and attach to rim joists,
using deck screws.
2. Verify the measurements,
mark, and cut the landing
face boards (O) to length. Position top edges flush with
decking and attach to landing
rim joist, using deck screws.

BUILD THE RAILING.
1. Measure, mark and cut the
railing posts (P) to length (see
Railing Detail, above).
2. At the bottom of each post,
counterbore two holes ½"
deep, using a spade bit slightly
larger than the diameter of the
washers.
3. Drill two ¼" pilot holes
through the bottom of each
post. Position posts (see *Face
Board Detail*, above), mark

Drill ⅛" pilot holes, then screw the top rail sections together where they meet at the corners.

After attaching angle brackets, turn stringers upside down and install treads, using 1¼" lag screws.

and drill pilot holes in deck, and attach to the face board and rim joist, using lag screws.

4. Cut each top rail section (R) the same length as the face board below it. Miter the ends of each section at 22½°.

5. Fasten the top rails to the posts with screws.

6. Measure, mark and cut railing balusters (Q) to length.

7. Drill ⅛" pilot holes in the balusters, and attach them to the face boards and the top rails with screws.

8. To strengthen the corners, drill ⅛" pilot holes at an angle and screw the top rail sections together **(Photo H).**

9. Verify the measurements for the railing cap sections (S), and cut them to length with 22½° miters where the ends

meet. Attach to the posts and top rail with deck screws.

BUILD THE STAIRWAYS.
1. Measure, mark and cut the stringers (T) to size (see *Landing & Stairway Detail,* page 46).

2. Using a framing square, lay out the top step with a 6" rise (the top of the stringer is installed 1" below the surface of the decking) and 12" run. Extend the rise line to both edges of the stringer, and cut along this line.

3. Lay out the bottom step with a 7" rise and a 12¾" run. At the end of the run, draw a perpendicular line 7" long and make a mark. Draw another perpendicular line to the bottom edge of the stringer and cut to size (see *Landing & Stairway Detail,* page 46).

4. Position the angle brackets in place and attach to the stringers, using 1¼" lag screws.

5. Measure, mark and cut the treads (U) to length, and attach to the stringers with lag screws through the angle brackets, leaving a ⅛" gap between treads **(Photo I).**

6. Install the stairways by propping them in position against the landing and drilling ¼" pilot holes through the rim joists and face boards into the top end of the stringers. Attach with a pair of lag screws at each stringer.

LAY THE LANDING DECKING.
After installing the stairways, cut the landing decking (N) to length and attach with deck screws.

Wraparound Deck

Combine multiple seating possibilities with an expansive view.

By wrapping around an outside corner of your house, this versatile deck increases your living space and lets you take advantage of views in several directions. The plan also creates two symmetrical areas for sitting or relaxing, providing space for two distinct activities. Our plan also calls for a front stairway for easy access to your yard or garden. The horizontal rails and notched posts provide striking visual elements that enhance the deck's overall design and add to its intimate nature. By adding a box or rail planter (see *Deck Furnishings*, pages 78 to 81), you can bring your garden right up to the deck.

Cutaway View

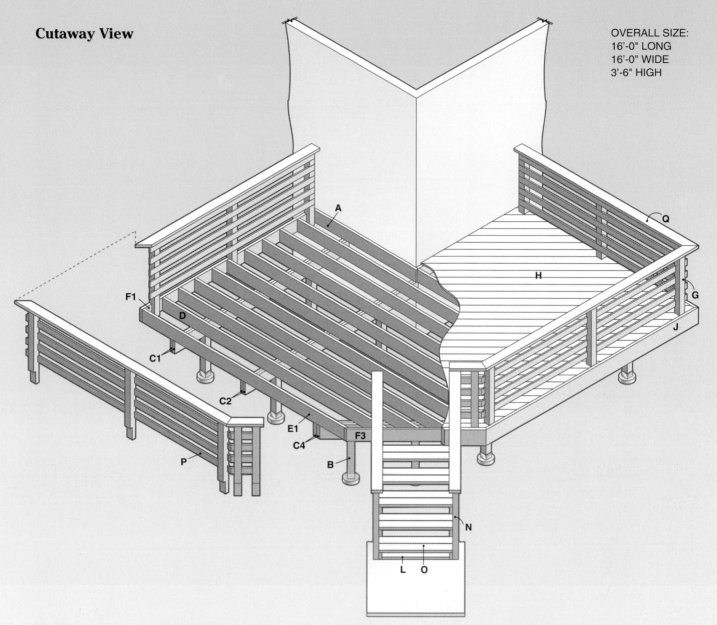

OVERALL SIZE:
16'-0" LONG
16'-0" WIDE
3'-6" HIGH

Lumber List			
Qty.	Size	Material	Part
9	2 × 8" × 16'	Trtd. Lumber	Joists (D)
6	2 × 8" × 12'	Trtd. Lumber	Ledgers (A), Beam boards (C), End joist (E), Rim joist (F)
13	2 × 8" × 10'	Trtd. Lumber	Beam boards (C), Joists (D), End joist (E), Rim joists (F), Lower gusset (L)
1	2 × 6" × 4'	Trtd. Lumber	Stairway nailer (I)
1	2 × 4" × 4'	Trtd. Lumber	Upper gusset (L)
3	4 × 4" × 8'	Trtd. Lumber	Deck posts (B)
9	4 × 4" × 8'	Cedar	Deck railing posts (G), Stairway railing posts (N)

Lumber List			
Qty.	Size	Material	Part
28	⁵⁄₄ × 6" × 16'	Cedar	Decking (H)
2	2 × 10" × 12'	Cedar	Face boards (J)
2	2 × 10" × 10'	Cedar	Face boards (J)
1	2 × 10" × 6'	Cedar	Face boards (J)
1	2 × 12" × 12'	Cedar	Stringers (K)
5	2 × 6" × 12'	Cedar	Railing cap (Q)
5	2 × 6" × 8'	Cedar	Treads (O)
10	1 × 4" × 12'	Cedar	Rails (P)
11	1 × 4" × 10'	Cedar	Rails (P)
8	1 × 4" × 6'	Cedar	Rails (P)

Supplies: 8"-diameter footing forms (8); J-bolts (8); 4 × 4" metal post anchors (8); post-beam caps (8); 90° 2 × 8" joist hangers (26); 45° 2 × 8" joist hangers (3); 1½ × 1½" galvanized metal angle brackets (26); joist hanger nails; ⅜ × 4" lag screws and washers (20); ⅜ × 3" lag screws and washers (32); 6 × 30" mending plate (1); silicone caulk (3 tubes); 3" masonry screws; 3" galvanized deck screws; 1½" galvanized deck screws; ⅝" galvanized screws; concrete as required.

Framing Plan

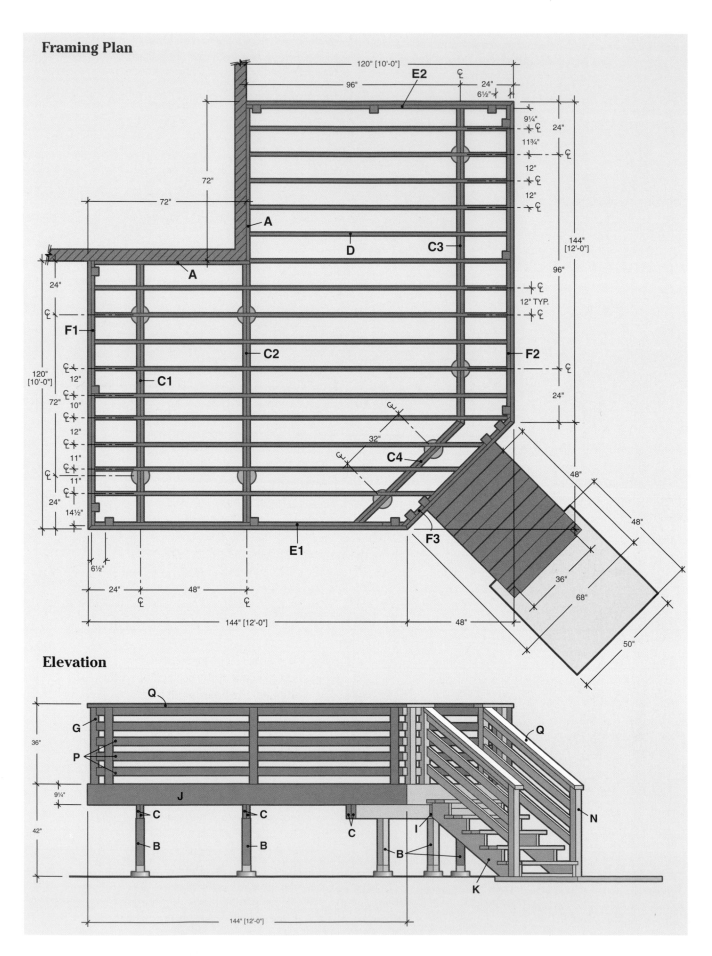

Elevation

Railing Detail

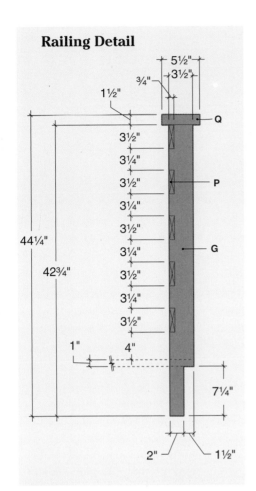

- 5½"
- 3½"
- ¾"
- 1½"
- Q
- 3½"
- 3¼"
- 3½"
- 3¼"
- P
- 3½"
- 3¼"
- G
- 3½"
- 3¼"
- 44¼"
- 42¾"
- 3½"
- 1"
- 4"
- 7¼"
- 2"
- 1½"

Stairway Detail

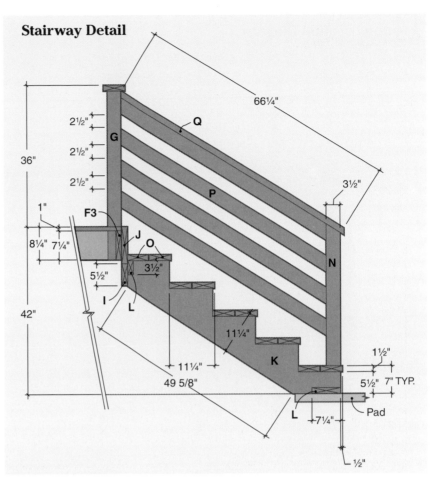

- 66¼"
- Q
- 2½"
- G
- 2½"
- 2½"
- P
- 3½"
- 36"
- 1"
- F3
- J
- O
- N
- 8¼" 7¼"
- 5½"
- 3½"
- I
- L
- 42"
- 11¼"
- 11¼"
- K
- 1½"
- 49 5/8"
- 5½" 7" TYP.
- L
- 7¼"
- Pad
- ½"

A

Attach the ledgers to the walls with ⅜ × 4" lag screws and washers, using a ratchet wrench.

Directions: Wraparound Deck

ATTACH THE LEDGERS.
1. Draw a level outline on the siding to show where the ledgers and the adjacent end joist and rim joist will fit against the house.
2. Position the top edge of the ledgers so that the surface of the decking boards will be 1" below the indoor floor level. This height difference prevents rainwater or melted snow from seeping into the house. Draw the outline long enough to accommodate the thickness of rim joist F-1 and end joist E-2.
3. Cut out the siding along the outline with a circular saw. To keep the blade from cutting the sheathing underneath the siding, set the blade depth to the same thickness as the sid-

Footing Location Diagram

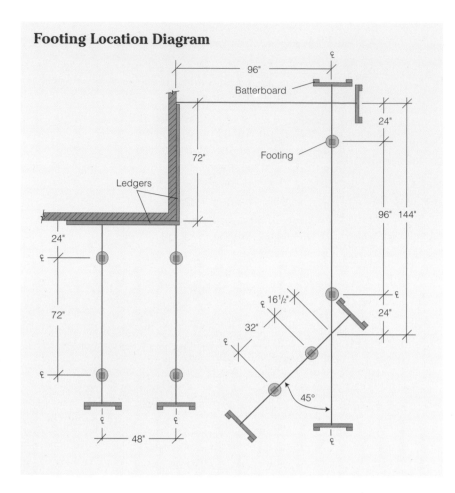

Set the post anchors in place, squaring them with the reference line scribed in the footings.

ing. Finish the corners of the cutout with a chisel, holding the beveled side in to ensure a straight cut.

4. Cut galvanized flashing to the length of the cutout, using metal snips, and slide the flashing up under the siding.

5. Measure and cut the ledgers (A) to length from pressure-treated lumber, using a circular saw. Remember, the ledger boards should be shorter than the overall length of the cutouts.

6. Position the ledgers in the cutout, underneath the flashing, and brace them in place. Fasten them temporarily with deck screws.

7. Drill pairs of ¼" pilot holes through the ledger and sheathing and into the house header joist at 2' intervals.

Counterbore each pilot hole ½" deep, using a 1" spade bit. Attach the ledgers to the wall with ⅜ × 4" lag screws and washers, using a ratchet wrench **(photo A).**

8. Apply a thick bead of silicone caulk between the siding and the flashing. Also seal the lag screw heads and any gaps between the wall and the ledger.

POUR THE FOOTINGS.

1. Referring to the *Footing Location Diagram* (above), stretch mason's strings across the site, using 2 × 4 batterboards. Check the mason's strings for square, using the 3-4-5 triangle method. From the point where each string meets the ledger, measure 3' along the ledger and make a mark.

Next, measure 4' out along the mason's string and mark with tape. The distance between the points on the ledger and the string should be 5'. If not, adjust the mason's strings accordingly. Measure along the strings to locate the centerpoints of the footings. Mark the locations with tape.

2. Drop a plumb bob at the tape locations and drive stakes into the ground to mark the centerpoints of the footings.

3. Remove the mason's strings and dig holes for the footings, using a clamshell digger or power auger.

4. Pour 2" to 3" of loose gravel into each hole for drainage. Make certain the hole dimensions comply with your local Building Code, which may require flaring the footings to 12" at the base.

5. Cut the footing forms to length, using a reciprocating saw or handsaw. Insert the forms into the holes, leaving 2" of each form above grade. Pack soil around the forms.

C

Use a speed square to mark a 22½° miter cut where the ends of beams C-3 and C-4 fit together.

INSTALL THE BEAMS.

1. Cut the beams from 2 × 10" lumber, adding several inches to each beam for final trimming. Position the beam boards (C) so the crowns face the same direction, and fasten them together with 10d galvanized nails spaced every 16".

2. Position beams C-1 and C-2 in their post-beam caps and attach them with nails.

3. Mark and cut the angled end of beam C-3 by mitering it at 22½° **(photo C).** Position the beam in the post caps.

4. Make a 22½° miter cut at one end of beam C-4 to form a 45° corner with beam C-3. Leave the other end long for final trimming. Place beam C-4 in the post-beam caps **(photo D).**

5. Fit the beams tightly together, fasten them with deck screws, and attach them to the post caps with nails.

6. Fill the forms with concrete and tamp the concrete with a long stick to eliminate any air pockets. Screed the tops flush with a flat 2 × 4. Insert a J-bolt into each footing, leaving ¾" to 1" of thread exposed.

7. Retie the mason's strings and drop a plumb bob to position each J-bolt at the exact center of the footing. Clean the bolt threads before the concrete sets.

SET THE DECK POSTS.

1. Start by laying a long, straight 2 × 4 flat across each pair of footings. With one edge tight against the J-bolts, draw a reference line across each footing.

2. Place a metal post anchor on each footing, center it over the J-bolt, and square it with the reference line **(photo B).** Thread a nut over each J-bolt

and tighten each of the post anchors in place.

3. Cut the posts (C) to their approximate length, adding several inches for final trimming. Place the posts in the anchors and tack them into place with one nail each.

4. With a level as a guide, use braces and stakes to plumb the posts. Once the posts are plumb, finish nailing them to the anchors.

5. To determine the height of the posts, make a mark on the house 7¼" down from the bottom edge of the ledger. Use a straight 2 × 4 and a level to extend this line across a post. Transfer this line to the remaining posts.

6. Cut the posts off with a reciprocating saw or a handsaw and attach post-beam caps to the tops, using 8d nails.

D

Fit beam C-4 tightly against beam C-3 and attach the two beams to each other with deck screws.

INSTALL THE JOISTS.

1. Referring to the *Framing Plan* on page 52, cut rim joist F–1 to final length, and cut end joist E-1 generously long, to allow for final trimming.

2. Fasten one end of rim joist F-1 to the ledger with 16d galvanized nails. Rest end joist E-1 in place on beams C-1 and C-2. Fasten F-1 and E-1 together with deck screws.

3. Use a framing square to finalize the location of E-1 on the beams. Mark the beams and trim them to length. Toenail E-1 in place on the beams.

4. Cut end joist E-2 to length. Install it by nailing it to the end of the ledger, checking for square, and toenailing it to the top of beam C-3. Trim the beam to length.

5. Mark the outlines of the inner joists (D) on the ledger, beams and rim joist F-1 (see *Framing Plan*, page 52), using a tape measure and a combination square.

6. Attach joist hangers to the ledger and rim joist F-1 with 1¼" joist hanger nails, using a scrap 2 × 8 as a spacer to achieve the correct spread for each hanger. NOTE: Spacing between the joists is irregular to accommodate the installation of railing posts.

7. Place the inside joists in the hangers on the ledger and on rim joist F-1, crown up, and attach them with 1¼" joist hanger nails. Be sure to use all the nail holes in the hangers. Toenail the joists to the beams and leave the joists long for final trimming.

8. Mark the final length of the inside joists by making a line across the tops of the joists from the end of end joist E-2. Check for square. Brace the in-

Mark the three remaining inside joists for cutting by snapping a chalk line. Brace and miter-cut the three inside joists.

side joists by tacking a board across their edges for stability. Cut them to length with a circular saw.

9. Cut rim joist F-2 long to allow for final trimming, and nail into position with 16d galvanized nails.

10. To mark the remaining joists for trimming at a 45° angle, make a mark 139" from the 90° corner on end joist E-1. Make a second mark 139" from the other 90° corner along rim joist F-2. The distance between these two points should be at least 70". If necessary, move the line back until it measures 70". Regardless of the overall dimensions of your deck, this length will ensure adequate space for mounting the railing posts at the top of the stairway.

11. Mark the last three joists for cutting by snapping a chalk line between the marked points on end joist E-1 and rim joist F-2 **(photo E).**

Transfer the cut marks to the faces of the joists with a combination square, and cut the miters with a circular saw.

12. Measure, cut and attach rim joist F-3 across the angle with deck screws.

INSTALL THE RAILING POSTS.

1. Cut the railing posts (G) to size and notch the lower ends to fit around the rim joists (see *Railing Detail*, page 53).

2. Clamp all but two of the posts together to lay out and cut ¾ × 3½" notches, or dadoes, for the horizontal rails. NOTE: The posts at the stairway are not notched for rails.

3. Cut the dadoes by making a series of parallel ¾"- deep cuts within each 3½" space, about ¼" apart, with a circular saw. Knock out the waste wood between the cuts, using a hammer. Then, chisel smooth the bottom of each dado.

4. To locate the railing posts

F

Drill pilot holes through the posts and into the rim joists, and attach the posts with lag screws. Note the unnotched stairway post.

on the diagonal corner, find the centerline of rim joist F-3 and measure 18" in both directions. These points are the inner faces of the railing posts and the outer faces of the stringers. Drill ¼" pilot holes through the railing posts into the rim joist, and secure the posts with lag screws.

5. To position the corner railing posts, measure 3" both ways from the outside corners of rim joist F-3. Predrill the posts, and use a ratchet wrench to attach them to the rim joists with lag screws **(photo F).**

6. Use the *Framing Plan*, page 52, and the *Corner Post Detail*, page 58, to locate the remaining railing posts.

INSTALL THE DECKING.
If possible, buy decking boards that are long enough to span the deck.

1. Measure, mark and cut the decking (H) to size, making

notches to fit around the railing posts. Position the first board above the stairway **(photo G),** and attach it by driving a pair of deck screws into each joist.

2. Position the remaining deck-

ing boards so that the ends overhang the deck, leaving a ⅛" gap between the boards to allow for drainage.

3. Where more than one board is required to span the deck, cut the ends at 45° angles and make the joint at the center of a joist.

4. Snap a chalk line flush with the edge of the deck, and cut off the overhanging ends of the deck boards with a circular saw set for a 1½"- deep cut.

INSTALL THE NAILER & FACE BOARDS.

1. Measure, mark and cut the stairway nailer (I) to size and attach it to the rim joist with a mending plate and deck screws (see *Stairway Detail,* page 53).

2. Measure, mark and cut the face boards (J) to length, making 45° miter cuts at the right angle corners and 22½° miter cuts at the stairway corners. Attach the face boards to the rim and end joists with pairs of deck screws at 2' intervals.

G

Cut the notches for the first decking board and position it above the stairway.

Drill ⅛" pilot holes through the treads to prevent splitting. Then, attach the treads to the stringers with deck screws, using a power driver.

Clamp the long rails, mark the ends, and transfer the lines across the face of the board with a combination square to ensure a tight-fitting 22½° miter with the short rail.

Corner Post Detail

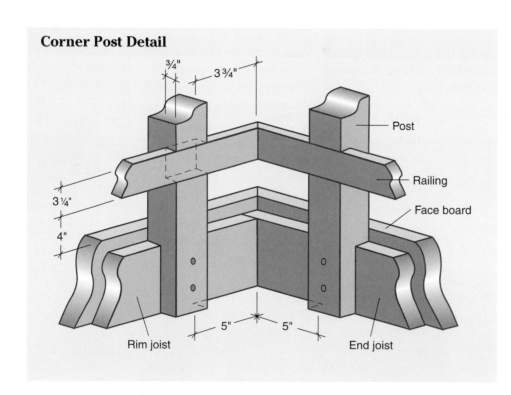

¾"
3 ¾"
Post
Railing
Face board
3 ¼"
4"
5"
5"
Rim joist
End joist

below the finished surface of the deck, to accommodate six 7" stairway rises. Stake the form into place.

4. Fill the form with concrete, screed it flush with a 2 × 4, and let the concrete set overnight.

BUILD THE STAIRWAY.
1. Lay out and cut the stringers (K) to size, according to the *Stairway Detail*, page 53. The center stringer is notched at the top and bottom to fit around the gussets. Mark the rises and runs with a framing square. Cut the notches with a circular saw, using a recipro-cating saw or handsaw to finish the corners.

2. Measure, mark and cut the gussets (L) to length. Assemble the stairway framework by nail-ing the gussets in place be-tween the outer stringers with 16d nails. Turn the framework upside down and attach the

POUR THE CONCRETE PAD.
1. Determine the location for the pad. Add 6" in each direc-tion, and excavate the area approximately 8" deep.

2. Lay and tamp a 4" base of compactable gravel.
3. Build a form from 2 × 6" lumber (see *Framing Plan*, page 52). Level the form at 42"

center stringer by nailing through the gussets.

3. Position the framework against the deck, and attach with deck screws driven through the upper gusset into the face board and nailer. Drill pilot holes through the lower gusset into the concrete pad; attach with masonry screws.

4. Cut the stairway railing posts (N) to length. To install the railing posts, clamp them in place against the stringers, drill pilot holes through the stringers into the posts, and attach the posts with ⅜ × 4" lag screws.

5. Measure, mark and cut the treads (O) to length. For the bottom treads, use a piece of railing post scrap to trace a line for the notch. Then, cut the notch with a circular saw. Attach the treads to the stringers with deck screws **(photo H).**

Use angle brackets to attach the stairway railing pieces and angled rails. To attach the brackets to the rails, use ⅝" galvanized screws.

BUILD THE RAILING.

1. Measure and cut to length the 10' rails, each with one end mitered at 45°. Install the rails, using 1½" deck screws.

2. Miter one end of the long rails at 45°. Leave the other end long for final trimming.

3. Clamp each long rail in place and use a straightedge to mark cut lines at the angled corner **(photo I).** Transfer this line to the face of each rail, using a combination square. Remove the rails and miter-cut the ends for the angled corners at 22½°.

4. Reposition the rails and attach them to the railing posts with 1½" deck screws.

5. Measure, mark and cut the short rails to length with one end mitered at 22½° and the other end cut square.

6. Fasten the ends of the short rails to the railing posts above

the stairway with angle brackets **(photo J).** Use ⅝" galvanized screws to attach the brackets to the rails and 1½" deck screws to attach them to the posts. Attach them to the notched post as well, using 1½" deck screws.

7. Measure, mark and cut the deck railing cap (Q), and install it with 3" deck screws.

BUILD THE
STAIRWAY RAILING.

1. To mark the stairway posts for trimming, hold the edge of a straight 2 × 4 across the deck post at the top of the stairs and the stairway post below. With the upper end of the 2 × 4 against the underside of the deck railing cap, and the 2 × 4 parallel to the stairway stringer, mark a cut line on the stairway post along the underside of the

2 × 4. Cut the post to length.

2. Repeat the process to mark and cut the other stairway post to length.

3. Measure, mark and cut the stairway railing caps (see *Stairway Detail*, page 53). Place a cedar 2 × 6 on top of the stairway posts, mark the angles for the ends, and cut to length, allowing for a 1" overhang at the end of the stairway.

4. Install the stairway railing caps with 3" deck screws.

5. To cut the stairway rails, hold each one tight against the bottom of the cap and mark the ends. Cut the rails to length so that they fit tight between the posts.

6. To install the rails, mark the positions of the rails on the posts and attach them with angle brackets, using ⅝" screws and 1½" deck screws.

Angled Deck

Give yourself a commanding view from this unique angled deck.

Expand your living space with style. This attractive deck makes creative use of simple geometry to achieve both practicality and pizzazz.

The railing adds interest, with its combination of vertical balusters, horizontal rails and shaped railing posts. And the straight staircase — anchored to a concrete pad for stability — provides direct, convenient access.

Though designed for construction at medium height on level ground, this deck uses heavy-duty posts, beams, joists and footings. By simply lengthening posts and modifying the stairway (see pages 108 to 109) it's readily adaptable for installation at a higher level or on a sloped site.

Cutaway View

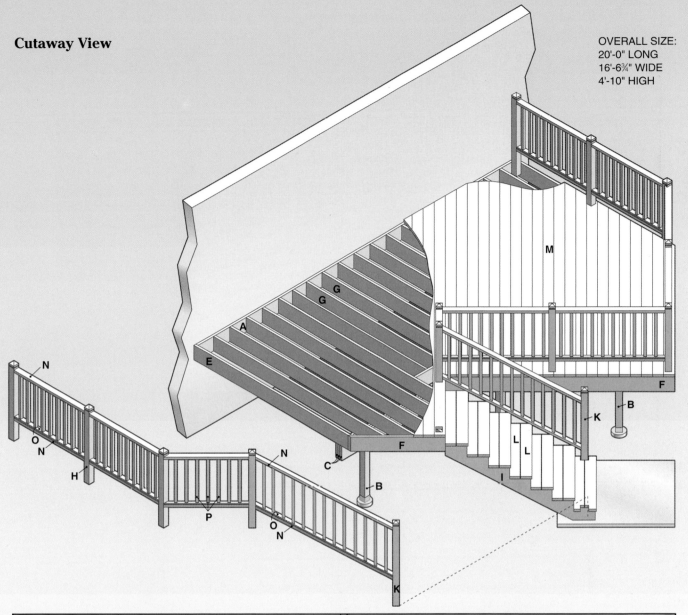

Lumber List			
Qty.	Size	Material	Part
4	2 × 10" × 20'	Trtd. lumber	Ledger (A), Primary beam boards (C)
1	2 × 10" × 18'	Trtd. lumber	Joists (G)
4	2 × 10" × 16'	Trtd. lumber	Joists (G)
5	2 × 10" × 14'	Trtd. lumber	Joists (G)
8	2 × 10" × 12'	Trtd. lumber	Joists (G)
5	2 × 10" × 10'	Trtd. lumber	Joists (G), End joists (E), Rim joists (F)
4	2 × 10" × 8'	Trtd. lumber	Secondary beam boards (D)
2	2 × 10" × 6'	Trtd. lumber	Rim joists (F)
2	6 × 6" × 8'	Trtd. lumber	Deck posts (B)

Lumber List			
Qty.	Size	Material	Part
1	2 × 6" × 8'	Trtd. Lumber	Gussets (J)
6	4 × 4" × 8'	Cedar	Railing posts (H)
4	4 × 4" × 10'	Cedar	Stair railing posts (K)
3	2 × 12" × 8'	Cedar	Stringers (I)
7	2 × 6" × 8'	Cedar	Treads (L)
38	2 × 6" × 16'	Cedar	Decking (M)
8	2 × 4" × 10'	Cedar	Top & bottom rails (N)
2	2 × 4" × 8'	Cedar	Top & bottom rails (N)
11	1 × 3" × 10'	Cedar	Top & bottom inner rails (O)
20	2 × 2" × 10'	Cedar	Balusters (P)

Supplies: 12"-diameter footing forms (4); J-bolts (4); 6 × 6" metal post anchors (4); 90° 2 × 10" joist hangers (22); 45° double 2 × 10" joist hangers (2); 3" galvanized deck screws; 1¾" galvanized deck screws; 3" masonry screws (4); joist hanger nails; 6d galvanized casing nails; ⅜ × 4" lag screws and washers (60); ⅜ × 5" carriage bolts, washers and nuts (22); silicone caulk (3 tubes); concrete as required.

Framing Plan

Post Detail

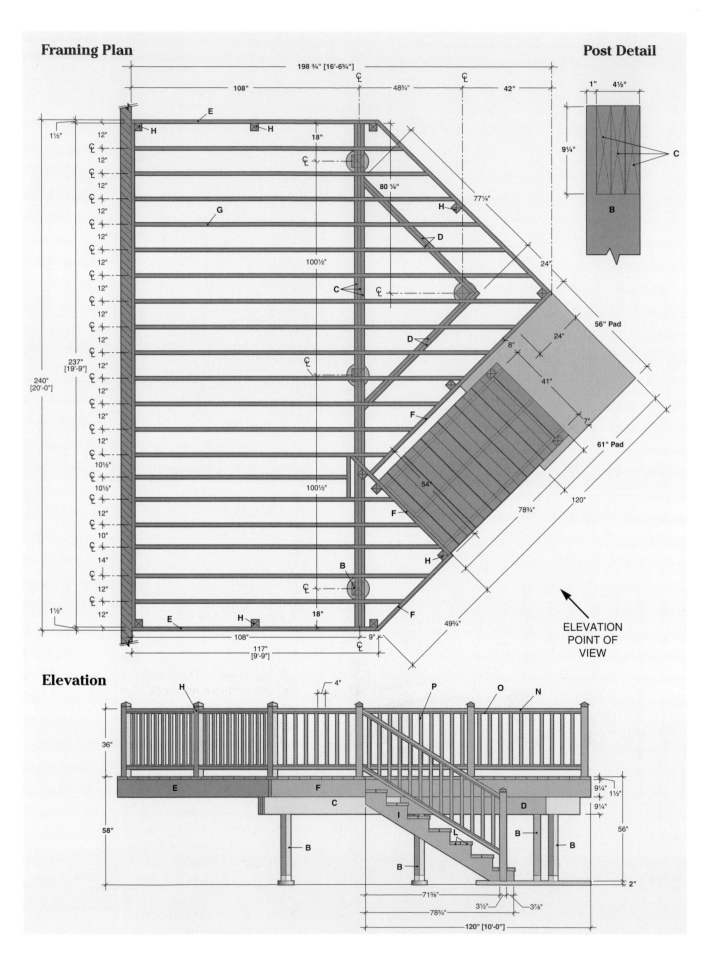

198 ¾" [16'-6¾"]

108" 48¾" 42"

E

H H H

12"

12" 18"

12"

12" 80 ¼" 77¼"

G H

12" D 24"

12" 100½" 56" Pad

12" 24"

12" C 8"

12" 56" Pad

12" 41" 7"

237" 12" D 61" Pad

[19'-9"] 12" F 54"

240" 12" 120"

[20'-0"] 12" 100½" 78¾"

10½" F

10½" 49¾"

12" H

10" B

14" 18"

12"

1½" E H 9"

12" 108" 117" [9'-9"]

1½"

ELEVATION POINT OF VIEW

1" 4½"

9¼"

C

B

Elevation

H 4" P O N

36"

9¼" 1½"

E F 9¼"

C D 56"

I

B L B

58" B

B

2"

71⅜" 3½" 3⅞"

78¾"

120" [10'-0"]

Railing Detail

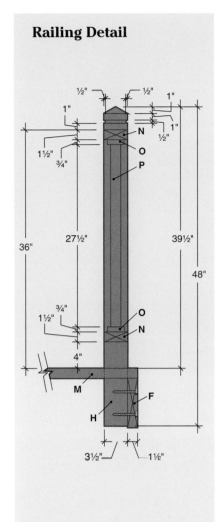

Stairway Detail

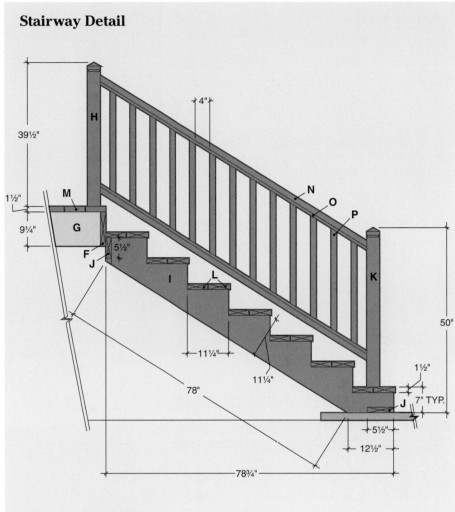

Directions: Angled Deck

ATTACH THE LEDGER. The ledger anchors the deck and establishes a reference point for building the deck square and level.

1. Draw a level outline on the siding to show where the ledger and the end joists will fit against the house. Install the ledger so that the surface of the decking boards will be 1" below the indoor floor level. This height difference prevents rainwater or melted snow from seeping into the house.

2. Cut out the siding along the outline with a circular saw. To

After attaching the ledger, drop a plumb line to a convenient height and stretch mason's strings. Mark footing locations with tape, and use the 3-4-5 triangle method to verify that the strings are square.

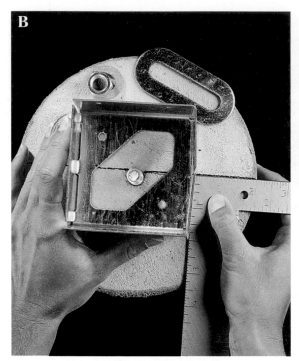

Square the post anchors to the reference lines on the top of each footing to ensure that the posts are aligned with each other.

Determine the finished post height by leveling a straight 2 × 4 from the bottom edge of the ledger.

prevent the blade from cutting the sheathing that lies underneath the siding, set the blade depth to the same thickness as the siding. Finish the cutout with a chisel, holding the beveled side in to ensure a straight cut.

3. Cut galvanized flashing to the length of the cutout, using metal snips. Slide the flashing up under the siding at the top of the cutout.

4. Measure and cut the ledger (A) from pressure-treated lumber. Center the ledger end to end in the cutout, with space at each end for the end joist.

5. Brace the ledger into position under the flashing. Tack the ledger into place with galvanized nails.

6. Drill pairs of ¼" pilot holes at 16" intervals through the ledger and into the house header joist. Counterbore each pilot hole ½", using a 1"

spade bit. Attach the ledger with lag screws and washers, using a ratchet wrench.

7. Apply a thick bead of silicone caulk between siding and flashing. Also seal lag

screw heads and the cracks at the ends of the ledger.

POUR THE FOOTINGS.
1. To locate the footings, drop a plumb bob from the end of

After marking the notches for the primary beam, cut out the tops of the posts with a circular saw and a handsaw.

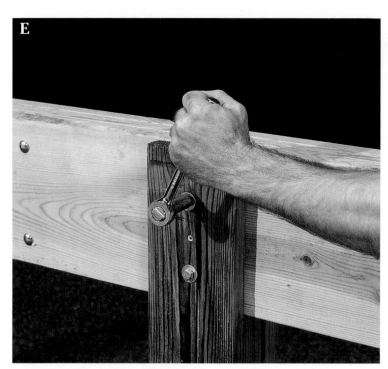

E

Use a ratchet wrench to tighten the lag screws that secure the primary beam to the notched posts.

the ledger down to a level that's comfortable for making measurements and stretching mason's strings.

2. Measurements for the footing centerpoints are shown on the *Framing Plan*, page 62. Construct, position and install temporary 2 × 4 batterboards.

3. Stretch three strings perpendicular to the house; one at each end of the ledger, and one at the centerline of the footing for the secondary beam, 80¼" from the right end of the ledger.

4. Make sure that the strings are square to the house **(photo A)** by using the 3-4-5 triangle method. Measuring from the point where the string meets the house, make a mark on the house at 3'. Then measure out along the string and make a mark at 4'. When the string is truly perpendicular, the diagonal line

connecting the two marked points will measure 5'. Adjust the string on the batterboard as needed.

5. Stretch the fourth string between batterboards, parallel to the house, at the centerline of the primary beam.

6. Measure along the parallel string and use tape to mark the three centerpoints of the footings for the primary beam.

7. To locate the footing for the secondary beam, use tape to mark a point on the middle perpendicular string that is 48¾" out from its intersection with the parallel string.

8. Transfer the locations to the ground by dropping a plumb bob from each tape mark and driving a stake into the ground at each point.

9. Remove the mason's strings and dig holes for the footings, using a clamshell digger or power auger. Pour

2" to 3" of loose gravel into each hole for drainage. NOTE: When measuring the footing size and depth, make sure you comply with your local Building Code, which may require flaring the base to 18".

10. Cut the footing forms to length, using a reciprocating saw or handsaw, and insert them into the footing holes, leaving 2" of tube above ground level. Pack soil around the forms for support, and fill with concrete, tamping with a long stick or rod to eliminate any air gaps.

11. Screed the tops flush with a straight 2 × 4. Insert a J-bolt into the center of each footing, leaving ¾" to 1" of thread exposed. Retie the mason's strings and use the plumb bob to position the J-bolts at the exact center of each footing. Clean the bolt threads before the concrete sets.

SET THE POSTS.

1. To provide a reference line for orienting the post anchors so the posts will be aligned with each other, lay a long, straight 2 × 4 flat across the primary beam footings, parallel to the ledger. With one edge tight against the J-bolts, draw a line across the top of each footing.

2. To mark the post anchor position on the footing for the secondary beam, mark a line across the footing at a 45° angle to the primary beam.

3. Place a metal post anchor on each footing, centering it over the J-bolt and squaring it with the reference line **(photo B).** Thread a nut over each J-bolt and securely tighten the post anchors in place.

After the secondary beam boards have been cut, assembled and attached with deck screws, secure the beam to the post with lag screws.

Cut the 45° angles on the ends of the joists with a circular saw.

4. Estimate the height of each post, and cut the posts slightly long to allow for final trimming. Set the posts in the anchors and tack into place with one nail.

5. With a level as a guide, use braces and stakes to ensure that the posts are plumb.

6. Determine the top of the posts by extending a straight 2 × 4 from the bottom edge of the ledger and marking a line on the posts level with the bottom of the ledger **(photo C).**

7. Outline a 4½ × 9¼" notch (see *Post Detail*, page 62) at the top of each of the primary-beam posts.

8. Remove the posts from the anchors, cut to finished height, and cut the notches, using a circular saw and handsaw **(photo D).**

9. Reposition the posts with the notches facing away from the house, brace them plumb and nail them securely to the post anchors.

INSTALL THE BEAMS.
We used 20' boards for the primary beam. However, for reasons of cost or availability, you may need to use 10'-long boards. Check with your local building inspector regarding acceptable joining hardware and techniques.

1. Construct the primary beam from 2 × 10" boards. Position the primary beam boards (C) so the crowns face the same direction, and fasten together with 16d galvanized nails. Drill pairs of ⅜" holes through the beam at 24" intervals, and secure with carriage

bolts, washers and nuts.

2. Measure, mark and cut the beam to length. Position the beam in the post notches, crown-side-up. Make sure the beam is square to the ledger by measuring the diagonals; adjust the beam position so the diagonal measurements are equal.

3. Drill two ¼" pilot holes through each post into the beam. Fasten with lag screws and washers, using a ratchet wrench **(photo E).**

4. Measure, mark and cut the post for the secondary beam slightly long to allow for final trimming. Install the post in the post anchor.

5. Locate and mark the points where the secondary beam butts against the primary beam. Run a straight 2 × 4 across the face of the post to the primary beam in both directions. Outline the ends of the secondary beam on the face of the primary beam, and install 45° 2 × 10 double joist hangers at each point.

6. Measure, mark and cut secondary beams boards (D) to length, using a circular saw.

7. Install the boards one at a time, verifying that they are level and attaching them with deck screws.

8. Drill pilot holes through the assembled beam and into the post. Counterbore the holes ½" deep with a 1" spade bit, and secure the secondary beam to the post with lag screws **(Photo F).**

9. Fasten the secondary beam to the joist hangers with 10d galvanized nails.

INSTALL THE JOISTS.

1. Measure and cut the end joists (E), leaving them several inches long for final trimming. Install by nailing into the ends of the ledger with 16d galvanized nails and toenailing to the top of the primary beam.

2. The joists are not all evenly spaced. Referring to the *Framing Plan*, use a combination square and draw the joist outlines on the face of the ledger and the top of the beams.

3. Install a joist hanger on the ledger at each location. Attach one flange of a hanger to one side of each outline, using joist hanger nails. Use a spacer cut from scrap 2 × 10" lumber to achieve the correct spread for each hanger, then fasten the remaining side flange with joist

hanger nails. Remove the spacer and repeat the procedure to install the remaining joist hangers.

4. Measure, mark and cut the joists (G), using a circular saw. Be sure to leave the joists long to accommodate final angled trimming. Place joists in hangers with crown side up and attach with nails. Align joists with the outlines on the top of the beam and toenail in place.

5. Snap chalk lines along the top edges of the joists (see *Framing Plan*, page 62) to mark the perimeter of the deck. All the angles are either 45° or 90°. Allow for the 1½" thickness of the rim joists. Extend the cutoff lines to the faces of the joists, and make the cuts, using a circular saw **(photo G).**

6. Referring to the *Framing*

Pour the concrete into the staircase pad form, and screed flush with a straight 2 × 4.

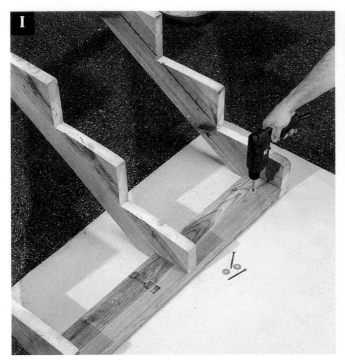

Drill pilot holes through the gusset and into the concrete pad, then attach with masonry screws, using a power drill.

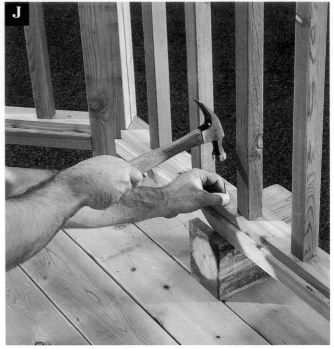

Use a nailing block to support the bottom rail, and attach the baluster assembly with nails. Notice the notch where the rails join the post at a 45° angle.

Plan and confirming the actual dimensions of your deck, measure, mark and cut the rim joists (F) to size and attach them to the joists with deck screws.

INSTALL THE RAILING POSTS. Locate railing posts in the corners of the deck, then center the intermediate posts between them (see *Framing Plan,* page 62).

1. Cut railing posts (H) to length (see *Railing Detail*, page 63). Cut a 60° pyramid on the top of each post, and rout a ½ × ½" groove on all four sides 1" below the pyramid.

2. To install the railing posts, clamp them one at a time into position, and drill ¼" pilot holes through the rim joist into the post. Counterbore the holes ½" using a 1" spade bit, and secure the posts to the rim joists with lag screws.

POUR THE PAD.

1. Determine the location of the concrete pad. Add 6" in each direction, and excavate approximately 8" deep.

2. Lay and tamp a 4" base of compactible gravel.

3. Build a form from 2 × 6" lumber, and align the inside of the form with the outside rim joists as shown in the *Framing Plan*, page 62. Level the form at 56" below the finished surface of the deck, to accommodate eight 7" stairway rises. Stake the form into place.

4. Fill the form with concrete, screed with a straight 2 × 4 **(photo H),** and let the concrete set up overnight.

INSTALL THE STAIRWAY.

1. Lay out the stringers (I), according to the *Stairway Detail*, page 63. Notch the center stringer at the top and bottom to fit around the gussets. Mark the rises and runs with a fram-

ing square. Cut the notches with a circular saw, using a reciprocating saw or handsaw to finish the corners.

2. Measure, mark and cut the gussets (J) to length. Assemble the stairway framework by nailing the gussets in place between the outer stringers with 16d nails. Turn the framework upside down and attach the center stringer by nailing through the gussets.

3. Position the stairway framework against the deck rim joist and attach with deck screws driven through the top gusset into the rim joist. Drill pilot holes through the bottom gusset into the concrete pad and attach with masonry screws **(photo I).**

4. Cut the stair railing posts (K) to length. Shape the top ends. Install the posts by clamping them into place against the stringers, drilling pilot holes through the stringers into the

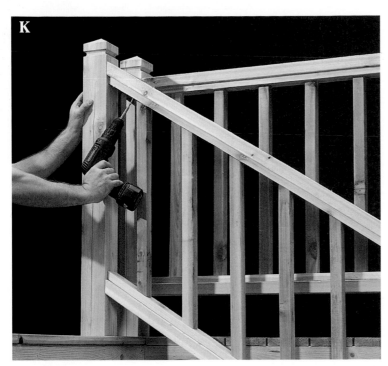

K

Drive deck screws up through the top inner rail to attach the top rail to the baluster assembly.

posts, and attaching with lag screws and washers.

5. Measure and cut the treads (L) to length, using a circular saw. The bottom treads are notched to fit around the posts.

INSTALL THE DECKING.

If possible, buy decking (M) long enough to span the deck. When joints between deck boards are necessary, center them above joists so the ends of both boards are supported.

1. Position the first deck board along the outer 45° rim joist, and mark the railing post locations. Cut notches for the railing posts, using a circular saw, handsaw and chisel. Attach the board by driving two deck screws into each joist.

2. Cut and attach the remaining deck boards, leaving a ⅛" gap between the boards for drainage.

INSTALL THE RAILING.

The railing for this deck is assembled in sections and then installed. The balusters are first fastened between the inner rails, then the baluster assembly is cut to exact length and attached to the outer rails.

1. Verify the measurements between your railing posts. Measure, mark and cut the top and bottom rails (N) to length.

2. Install the bottom rails by drilling angled ⅛" pilot holes into the posts at the ends, and attaching with deck screws. NOTE: Where the railings meet the posts at a 45° angle, you'll need to notch the ends to fit.

3. Measure, mark and cut the top and bottom inner rails (O), leaving them several inches long for final trimming.

4. Measure, mark and cut the deck balusters (P) to length.

5. Assemble each railing section by positioning the balusters between the top and bottom inner rails, drilling ⅛" pilot holes, and attaching them with deck screws. Trim the section to final length with an equal space at each end.

6. Position the baluster assembly on the bottom rail and nail in place **(photo J).**

7. Position the top rail above the baluster assembly, drill pilot holes through the top inner rail into the top rail, and attach with deck screws from below.

8. To determine the angle for the ends of the stairway rails and balusters, as well as the length of the inner and outer stairway rails, hold a straight 2 × 4 across one pair of stairway posts. With the top edge of the 2 × 4 crossing each post at the routed groove, mark the angle on the back of the board. NOTE: The angle will be approximately 32°, but you'll get the best fit by marking it from your actual railing posts.

9. Measure, mark and cut the top and bottom rails to length, with the ends angled to fit against the posts. Install the bottom rails.

10. Cut inner rails and balusters to size with mitered ends.

11. Build the stairway railing assemblies using the same procedures as used for the deck railing assemblies, taking care that the space between balusters is 4" or less.

12. Install the stairway railing assemblies by positioning them on the bottom rails and nailing with 6d casing nails.

13. Install the stairway top rails by positioning them above the railing assemblies, drilling pilot holes through the top inner rails and driving deck screws from below **(photo K).**

Low-Profile Deck

An attractive alternative to a plain patio.

This V-patterned decking directs your view to the centerpoint of the deck and creates a distinctive focal point to the ground-level entry. The decking treatment adds interest and a touch of elegance. A platform, or low-profile, deck like this one is ideal for flat, level lots or for covering up an old cement patio. This deck requires no posts, so construction is easier than building a higher deck. Since this deck is less than 30" high, there's also no requirement for a railing. This deck can hold a BBQ grill, table, chairs and our box planter and bench accessories (pages 78 to 85). Our plan also calls for a suspended step that's perfect for areas with snow and frost.

Cutaway View

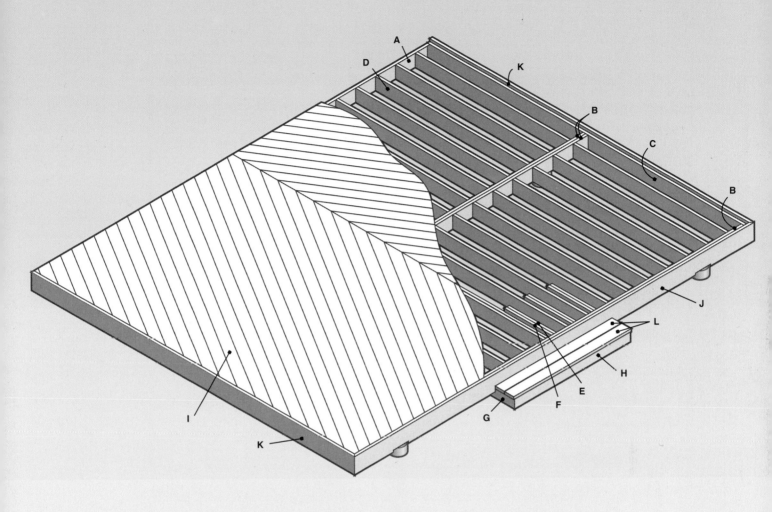

		Lumber List				Lumber List	
Qty.	Size	Material	Part	Qty.	Size	Material	Part
5	2 × 8" × 20'	Trtd. lumber	Ledger (A) & Beam bds (B)	1	2 × 6" × 6'	Cedar	End step supports (G)
2	2 × 8" × 16'	Trtd. lumber	End joists (C)	3	2 × 6" × 6'	Cedar	Step riser (H) & Tread (L)
40	2 × 8" × 8'	Trtd. lumber	Joists (D)	74	2 × 6" × 10'	Cedar	Decking (I)
3	2 × 4" × 8'	Trtd. lumber	Step support spacers (E)	1	2 × 10" × 20'	Cedar	Front face bd (J)
2	2 × 6" × 8'	Trtd. lumber	Interior step supports (F)	2	2 × 10" × 16'	Cedar	Side face bds (K)

Supplies: 8"-diameter footing forms (6); 3" direct bearing hardware (6); 2 × 8" double joist hangers (4); 2 × 8" joist hangers (72); 3" galvanized deck screws; joist hanger nails; 16d galvanized box nails; 12d galvanized casing nails; ⅜ × 4" carriage bolts, washers, and nuts (12); ⅜ × 4" lag screws (22); lead masonry anchors (22); ledger flashing (20'); exterior silicone caulk (3 tubes); concrete as required.

Framing Plan

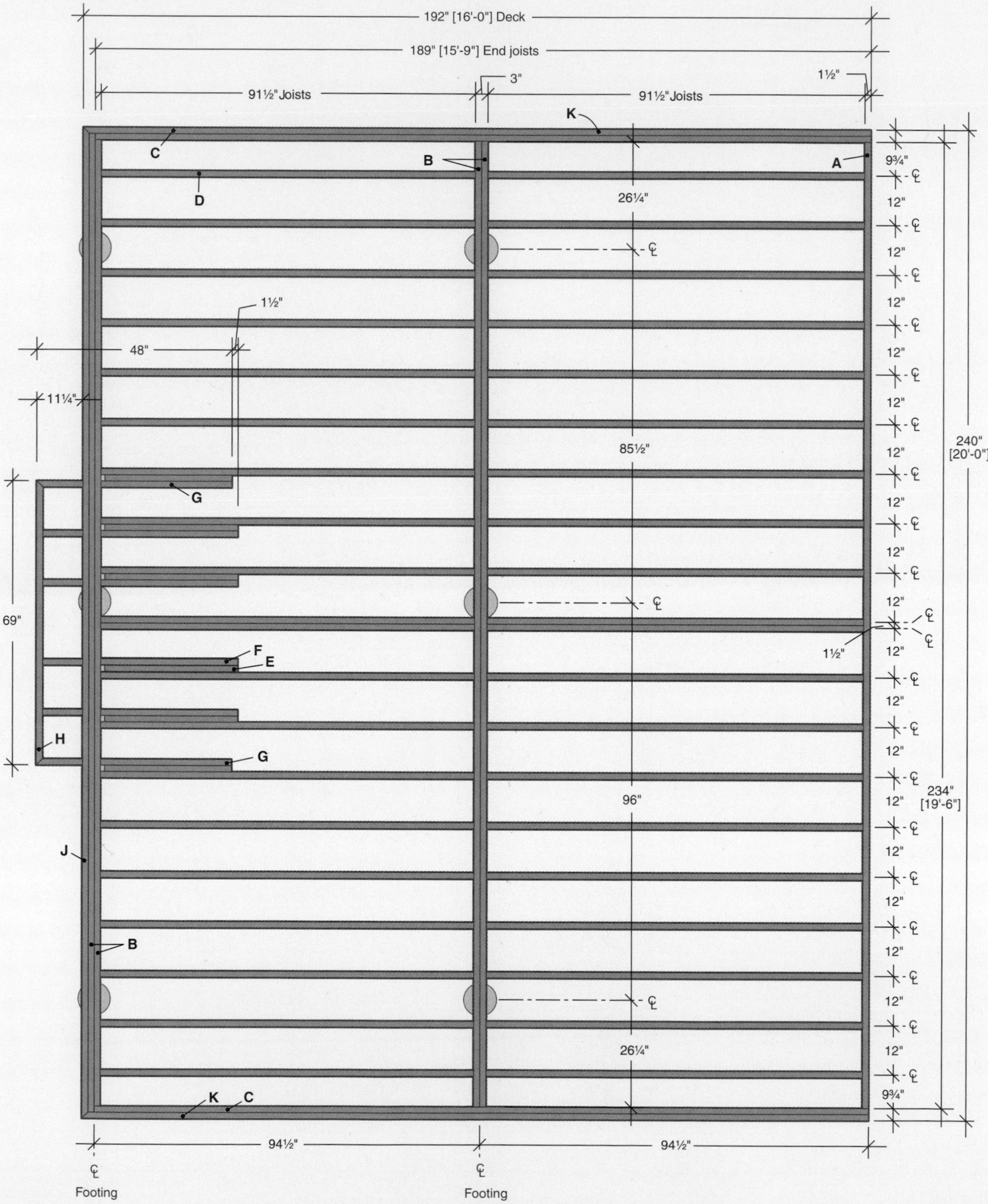

192" [16'-0"] Deck

189" [15'-9"] End joists

91½" Joists   3"   91½" Joists   1½"

K

C

B

A   9¾"

D   26¼"   12"

12"

12"

1½"

48"   12"

11¼"   12"

85½"   12"

12"

G   12"

69"   12"

1½"   12"

F   12"
E

H   G   12"

96"   12"

J   12"

12"

B   12"

12"

26¼"   12"

9¾"

K   C

94½"   94½"

C̶L   C̶L
Footing   Footing

240"
[20'-0"]

234"
[19'-6"]

Elevation and Details

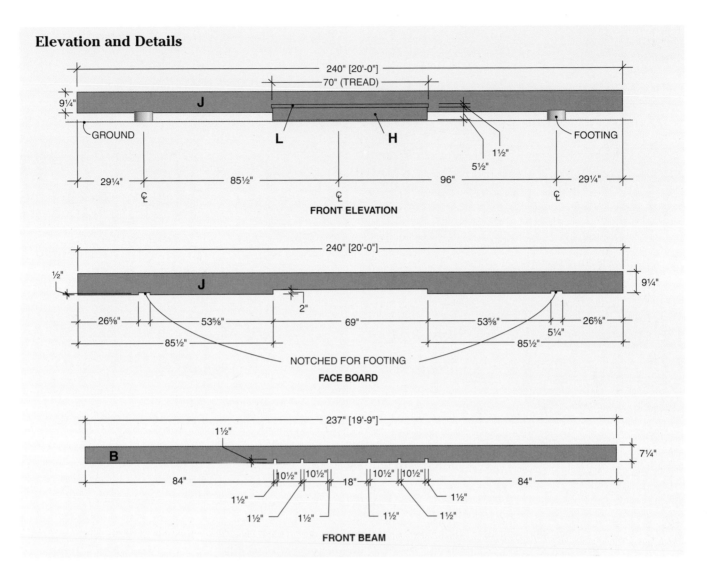

FRONT ELEVATION

240" [20'-0"]
70" (TREAD)
9¼"
J
GROUND
L
H
FOOTING
1½"
5½"
29¼"
85½"
96"
29¼"

FACE BOARD

240" [20'-0"]
½"
J
9¼"
26⅝"
53⅝"
2"
69"
53⅝"
5¼"
26⅝"
85½"
85½"
NOTCHED FOR FOOTING

FRONT BEAM

237" [19'-9"]
1½"
B
7¼"
84"
10½" 10½"
18"
10½" 10½"
84"
1½"
1½"
1½"
1½"
1½"

Directions: Low-Profile Deck

ATTACH THE LEDGER.

1. Measure and cut the ledger (A) to length. Drill pairs of ¼" pilot holes at 2-ft. intervals. Counterbore each hole ½", using a 1" spade bit.

2. Determine ledger location and draw its outline on the wall. Make sure you include a 3" space at each end of the ledger for the end joists and side face boards. Temporarily brace the ledger in position, using 2 × 4s. Make sure the ledger is level and mark the hole locations on the wall with an awl or nail.

Attach the ledger to the masonry wall with lag screws and washers, using a ratchet wrench.

Stretch level mason's strings between the bottom of the ledger and temporary batterboards. Level the footing forms against the strings.

Set the direct-bearing hardware into the wet concrete, using layout strings to ensure accurate alignment.

3. Remove the ledger and drill anchor holes 3" deep, using a ⅜" masonry bit. Drive lead anchors into the drilled holes, using a rubber mallet, and attach the ledger to the wall with lag screws and washers, using a ratchet wrench. **(Photo A).**

4. Seal the screw heads, and the joint between the wall and ledger, with silicone caulk.

POUR THE FOOTINGS.

1. To locate the footings, refer to the measurements in the *Framing Plan* (page 72) and mark the centerline for each pair of footings on the ledger.

2. Construct three temporary 2 × 4 batterboards. Position the batterboards out from the footing marks, approximately 19 feet from the ledger.

Stretch mason's string from the bottom of the ledger at each mark to the corresponding batterboard, making sure the strings are level and perpendicular to the ledger.

3. Check for square, using the 3-4-5 triangle method. From the point where each string meets the ledger, measure 3' along the ledger and make a mark. Next, measure 4' out along the string and mark with tape. The distance between the points on the ledger and the string should be 5'. If it's not, adjust the string position on the batterboard accordingly.

4. To locate the centers of the six footings, build four more batterboards and stretch two additional mason's strings parallel to the house (refer to the

Framing Plan on page 72 for measurements). Use a plumb bob to transfer the footing centerpoints to the ground, and drive a stake to mark each point.

5. Remove the mason's strings and dig the footings, using a clamshell digger or power auger. Pour 2" to 3" of loose gravel into each footing hole for drainage. NOTE: When measuring the footing size and depth, make sure you comply with your local Building Code, which may require flaring the base to 12".

6. Cut the footing forms to length, using a reciprocating saw or handsaw, and insert them into the footing holes.

7. Retie the mason's strings, making sure they are level.

8. Level the tops of the forms

Set the beams in the direct-bearing hardware on the footings. Note the "notch" for the end joist at the end of the outer beam.

Measure, cut and install the joists with joist hangers, verifying the length of each one as you go.

by setting them flush with the mason's strings **(Photo B)** and packing soil around them to hold them securely in place.

9. Remove the mason's strings and fill the footing forms with concrete, tamping with a long stick or rod to eliminate any air gaps.

10. Screed the concrete flush with a straight 2 × 4, and insert direct-bearing hardware into each footing while the concrete is still wet. Reattach the layout strings to ensure that the hardware is aligned correctly **(Photo C).**

INSTALL THE BEAMS.

1. Measure, mark and cut the beam boards (B) to length, using a circular saw. NOTE: Three of the beam boards are the same length as the ledger.

The fourth board is 3" longer to accommodate the 1½" end joist on each end.

2. Make each beam by fastening two beam boards together with pairs of box nails driven at 16" intervals. At both ends of the outer beam, the long beam board overhangs 1½", creating a notch for attaching the end joist.

3. Position the beams crown-side-up on the direct-bearing hardware **(Photo D).** Double-check that both beams are correctly aligned with the ledger, and attach to the hardware with carriage bolts.

INSTALL THE JOISTS.

1. Measure, mark and cut the end joists (C) to length. The end joists extend from the house to the notch in the end of the outer beam. In our plan the end joists are 189" long, but verify this measurement before cutting. Attach the end joists to the ledger and beams with box nails.

2. Measure, mark and cut double center joists (D). Mark the centerline of the deck on the ledger and beams, install double joist hangers at each mark, and nail the joists in place. Seal the seam between the beam boards in the double joists with silicone caulk. to protect against moisture.

3. Locate the remaining joists by measuring along the ledger and beams from the center joists, and marking centerlines at 12" intervals (see *Framing Plan*). Install a joist hanger at each centerline.

4. Measure, mark and cut the inner joists (D), verifying the actual lengths, and install in joist hangers with joist nails **(Photo E).**

Cut 1½ × 1½" notches for the step supports in the outer beam with a reciprocating saw or handsaw. Finish the notches with a hammer and chisel.

Lay the decking boards with a ⅛" space to provide for drainage. Leave the boards slightly long to allow for trimming after installation.

BUILD THE STEP.

Our plan includes a cantilevered step suspended from the underside of the deck. This step is constructed with 2 × 6 step supports (F, G) attached to the lower portions of the deck joists. Notches in the bottom edge of the outer beam (see *Detail*, page 73) allow the supports to run through. A long notch in the front face board (see *Detail*, page 73) accommodates all the step supports. Spacers (E) offset the step supports from the joists to avoid the joist hangers.

1. Measure, mark and cut the step support spacers (E). Set the spacers back approximately 1" from the front beam, and attach to the deck joists with deck screws (see *Step Detail,* page 77).

2. Cut 1½" × 1½" notches in the bottom edge of the front beam, adjacent to the step support spacers. Use a reciprocating saw or handsaw to make the vertical cuts, and finish each notch with a chisel and hammer **(Photo F).**

3. Measure, mark and cut the step supports (F) and end step supports (G) to length. Make a 45° miter cut at the front of the end step supports where they meet the step riser. Attach the step supports to the spacers with deck screws. The interior step supports extend 11¼" beyond the beam, while the end step supports extend 12¾" to allow for the miter joints at the riser.

4. Measure, mark and cut the step riser (H) to length, with 45° mitered ends. Attach the riser to the step supports with casing nails.

LAY THE DECKING.

Dimension lumber is not always perfectly straight and true, so we snapped 45° chalk reference lines to ensure the accuracy of our diagonal decking pattern.

1. To create reference lines, mark a point in the center of the front of the deck. Measure equal distances along the double center joist, and along the outer beam. Mark a line between these points. As you progress with rows of decking, periodically measure between the ends of the decking boards and the reference line to help you maintain a consistent angle.

2. Begin laying the decking at the front center of the deck. Cut one end of the first decking board at a 45° angle and leave the other end slightly long. Position it above the step, aligning the 45° cut with the centerline of the double joist, and nail in place with casing nails.

3. Cut and attach the next deck board in similar fashion, leaving a ⅛" space between the boards.

4. Cut and attach the remaining deck boards **(Photo G),** periodically checking the angle of the decking against the reference lines and making any necessary adjustments.

5. After installing the decking, snap another chalk line flush with the outside face of the outer beam and end joists. Set the blade depth on your circular saw at slightly more than 1½", and trim the decking to the line.

Step Detail

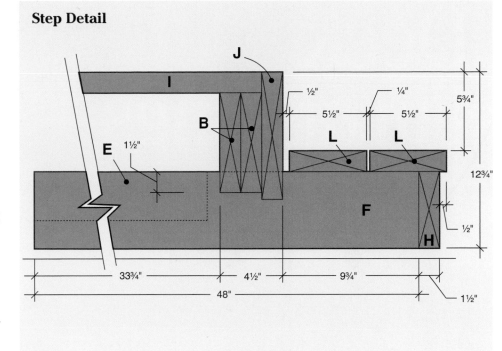

INSTALL THE FACE BOARDS.
1. Measure, mark and cut the front face board (J) to size (see *Detail,* page 73), and notch it to fit around the step supports. Cut 45° miters on both ends.

2. Temporarily clamp the face board in place and mark for notching around the footings. Also mark the points where the carriage bolts in the direct-bearing hardware contact the back of the board.

3. Remove the board, cut the footing notches, and chisel out the back of the board to accommodate the carriage bolts. Attach the face board with casing nails.

4. Measure, mark and cut the side face boards (K) to length, making 45° miter cuts at the front ends. Attach the face boards to the end joists with deck screws.

INSTALL THE STEP TREADS.
Complete the suspended step by cutting the treads (L) to length and attaching them to the step supports, using casing nails. Leave a ½" gap at the front face board, and a ¼" gap between the treads **(Photo H).**

Cut step treads to length and attach with nails, leaving a ½" gap between the first tread and the face board.

Deck Furnishings

Elements that add personal style and charm to your deck

Lumber for arbor provided by P & M Cedar Products, Inc.

OVERALL SIZE:
16" HIGH
18" WIDE
48" LONG

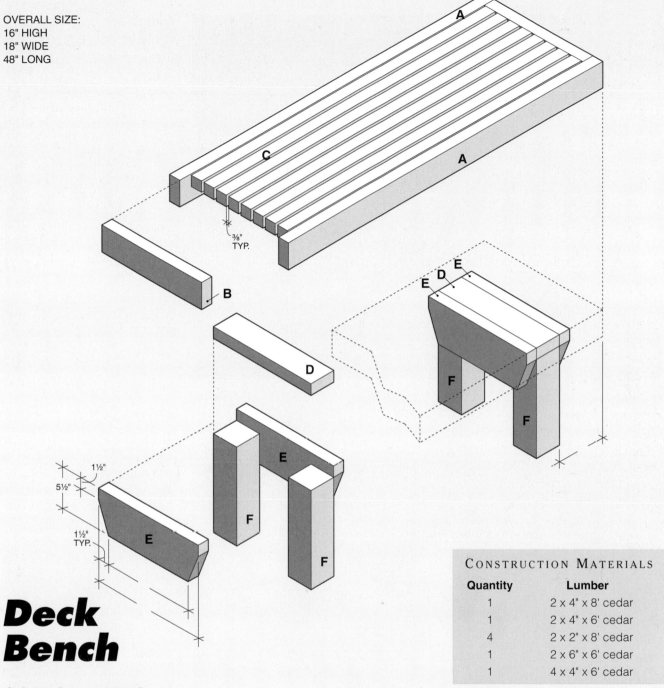

Deck Bench

A handsome and comfortable bench that's easy to make.

D ue to its modular design, this bench can be mixed or matched with planters or other benches. Cedar wood enables this bench to withstand sun, rain, and even snow. This bench will enhance your enjoyment of your deck and its beauty.

CONSTRUCTION MATERIALS

Quantity	Lumber
1	2 x 4" x 8' cedar
1	2 x 4" x 6' cedar
4	2 x 2" x 8' cedar
1	2 x 6" x 6' cedar
1	4 x 4" x 6' cedar

Cutting List

Key	Part	Dimension	Pcs.	Material
A	Sides	1½ x 3½ x 48"	2	Cedar
B	Ends	1½ x 3½ x 15"	2	Cedar
C	Slats	1½ x 1½ x 45"	8	Cedar
D	Stretchers	1½ x 3½ x 15"	2	Cedar
E	Braces	1½ x 5½ x 15"	4	Cedar
F	Legs	3½ x 3½ x 13"	4	Cedar

Supplies: 3" gold-colored deck screws (60), 2½" gold-colored deck screws (16).

Note: Measurements reflect the actual thickness of dimensional lumber.

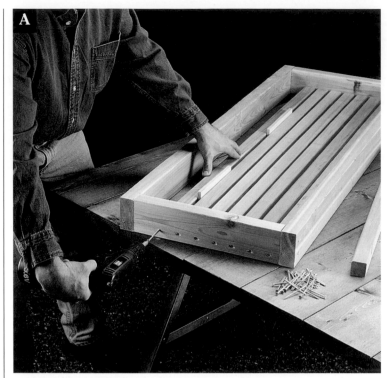

Use spacers to help you position the slats. Then, holding each slat firmly against the spacers, secure the slats with 3" screws driven through pilot holes.

With the stretchers positioned between the reference lines, attach the stretcher to each slat using 2½" screws.

Directions:
Deck Bench

MAKE THE FRAME.
The butt joints make this bench sturdy and easy to construct. For strength and good looks, we used gold-colored deck screws.

1. Measure, mark and cut the sides (A) and ends (B) to length, using a circular saw.

2. Position the ends between the sides so the edges are flush. Measure from corner to corner. When the diagonals are equal the frame is square.

3. Drill ⅛" pilot holes through the sides and into the ends. Fasten the sides to the ends by driving 3" gold-colored screws through the pilot holes.

BUILD THE SEAT.
The slats that make up the seat are spaced ⅜" apart to allow rain water to run off.

1. Cut the slats (C) to length using a circular saw.

2. Set the frame on a flat surface and place ⅜" spacers against one side. Place the first slat in the frame against the spacers. Drill ⅛" pilot holes through both ends into the slat. Secure the slat to the ends with 3" deck screws. Repeat this process of positioning and attaching slats until all the slats are in place **(photo A).**

3. Measure, mark and cut the stretchers (D) to length.

4. To mark the stretcher outlines, measure in 5" and 3½" from the inside of each end piece on the back of the slats and make a mark.

5. Position the stretchers between the marks. Drill ⅛" pilot holes through the stretchers into the slats. Attach the stretchers with 2½" screws **(photo B).**

ASSEMBLE THE BENCH.

The braces hold the legs in place against the stretchers.

1. Measure, mark and cut the braces (E) to length.

2. To shape the ends of each brace, mark the angle by measuring down 1½" from the top edge and 1½" along the bottom edge. Draw a line between the two end points and cut along that line **(photo C)**. Repeat this step at the other end of the brace.

3. On each brace, measure down ¾" from the top edge and draw a reference line across the stretcher for the screw positions. Drill ⅛" pilot holes along the reference line. Position a brace on each side of the stretchers and fasten it with 3" screws driven through the braces and into the stretchers.

4. Measure, mark and cut the legs (F) to length, using a circular saw. If needed, finish any cuts with a handsaw.

5. Position each leg between the braces and against the sides of the bench frame. Drill pilot holes through each brace and attach the leg to the braces by driving 3" screws through the braces and into the leg. Repeat the process for each leg until all legs are installed **(photo D)**.

APPLY THE FINISHING TOUCHES.

1. Sand all surfaces with 150-grit sandpaper. Be sure to sand edges thoroughly so bare legs will not be scratched.

2. Because cedar is naturally resistant to decay, it will age to a natural gray. To preserve its reddish color, you can apply a clear sealer as we did. Cedar is also suitable for painting.

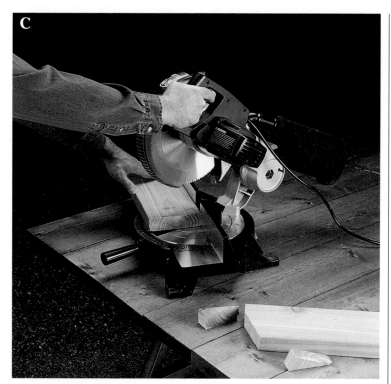

Measure and mark the angles on the braces, then cut the angles using a circular saw or a power miter saw.

Position each leg between the braces and against the sides. The legs are fastened to the braces with 3" screws.

OVERALL SIZE:
24½" HIGH
18¾" WIDE
18¾" LONG

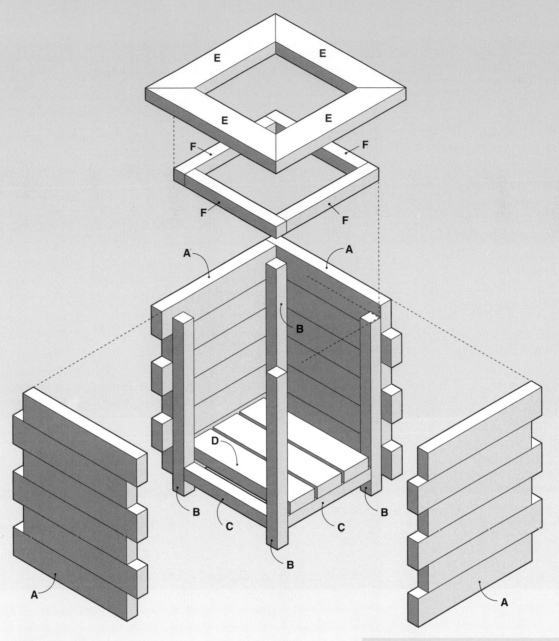

Box Planter

The versatile design of this planter offers a variety of uses.

This planter is large enough to hold a potted shrub, mixed flowers or even a miniature herb garden. The "tiered" construction process makes it both easy to build and sturdy enough for years of use.

CONSTRUCTION MATERIALS

Quantity	Lumber
8	2 × 4" × 6' cedar
3	2 × 2" × 6' cedar

Cutting List

Key	Part	Dimension	Pcs.	Material
A	Side	1½ × 3½ × 16½"	24	Cedar
B	Stringer	1½ × 1½ × 21½"	4	Cedar
C	Bottom cleat	1½ × 1½ × 12"	4	Cedar
D	Bottom	1½ × 3½ × 14¾"	3	Cedar
E	Frame	1½ × 3½ × 18¾"	4	Cedar
F	Top cleat	1½ × 1½ × 13¼"	4	Cedar

Supplies: 2½" gold-colored deck screws (120), 10d casing nails (10).

Note: Measurements reflect the actual thickness of dimensional lumber.

Place spacers into the corners of the first tier, stand the stringers on end, and attach, using deck screws.

Drill pilot holes through the bottom cleats, and attach with deck screws.

Directions: Box Planter

This planter is assembled upside down. The rows of side pieces, or tiers, are constructed independently, then stacked on top of each other and fastened together from the inside through the stringers.

1. Measure, mark and cut the side pieces (A) to length from 2 × 4" cedar stock.

2. Drill a pair of ⅛" pilot holes through each side piece, about ¾" from one end.

3. Form each of the six tiers by screwing four side pieces together with deck screws driven through the pilot holes.

4. Measure, mark and cut the stringers (B) to length.

5. Lay the first tier on a flat worksurface, then position a stringer upright in one corner using a scrap of 2 × 2" lumber as a spacer to raise the stringer off the worksurface.

6. Drill ⅛" pilot holes and attach the stringer to the tier with 2½" deck screws. Attach the other three stringers in the same fashion **(photo A).**

7. Add the remaining tiers one at a time, positioning each tier so the butt joints do not line up with those of the previous tier. Drill ⅛" pilot holes and attach each tier to the stringers with deck screws as you go.

8. Measure, mark and cut the bottom cleats (C) to length from 2 × 2" cedar stock.

9. With the planter box still upside down, position a bottom cleat between two stringers, so the edge of the cleat is flush with the edge of the side.

10. Drill angled ⅛" pilot holes, and attach the bottom cleat to the side using deck screws. Attach the remaining bottom cleats in the same fashion **(photo B).**

11. Measure, mark and cut bottom pieces (D) to length from 2 × 4" cedar stock.

12. Turn the box assembly right-side-up, and set the bottom pieces into the planter so they rest on the cleats and are evenly spaced.

13. Attach the bottom pieces by drilling pilot holes and driving deck screws through the bottom pieces into the cleats.

14. Measure, mark and cut the frame pieces (E) from 2 × 4" cedar stock, mitering the ends at 45°.

15. Dry-fit the frame pieces together, with the miter joints tight. Join the frame pieces with casing nails.

16. Cut top cleats (F) to size from 2 × 2" cedar stock. Position the cleats on the assembled frame so the edges are flush with the inside edge of the framing pieces. Drill pilot holes through the cleats and attach by driving deck screws through the cleats into the frame.

17. Position the frame on the planter so the cleats fit tightly inside box. Attach the frame by drilling pilot holes and driving deck screws through the inside face of the top cleats.

18. Soften the corners and edges of the box planter with a rasp, then apply a finish of your choice; our planter is protected with a coat of clear sealant-preservative.

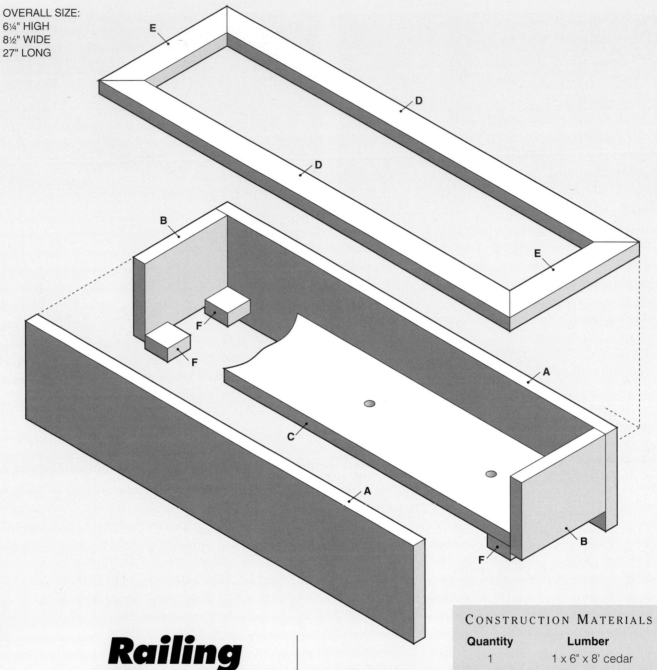

OVERALL SIZE:
6¼" HIGH
8½" WIDE
27" LONG

Railing Planter

Grow flowers or herbs in this sturdy cedar planter.

Though this planter is built with inexpensive ¾" cedar, adding a planter to your deck will add a touch of class. Build a few planters and create an attractive, colorful privacy hedge.

CONSTRUCTION MATERIALS

Quantity	Lumber
1	1 x 6" x 8' cedar
1	1 x 2" x 8' cedar

Cutting List

Key	Part	Dimension	Pcs.	Material
A	Sides	¾ × 5½ × 25½"	2	Cedar
B	Ends	¾ × 4⅜ × 5½"	2	Cedar
C	Bottom	¾ × 5½ × 24"	1	Cedar
D	Frame sides	¾ × 1½ × 27"	2	Cedar
E	Frame ends	¾ × 1½" × 8½"	2	Cedar
F	Feet	¾ × 1½ × 1½"	4	Cedar

Supplies: 6d finishing nails (26), 4d finishing nails (28).

Note: Measurements reflect the actual thickness of dimensional lumber.

Assemble the box by predrilling the sides and attaching them to the ends with 6d finishing nails.

After attaching the feet to the bottom, insert the bottom into the planter box so it is flush with the reference line. Fasten with 6d finishing nails.

Directions:
Railing Planter

The railing planter is designed with longer sides to fit over a standard size railing. Feet are installed to keep the planter off the railing and allow water to drain and air to circulate.

1. Measure, mark and cut the sides (A) and ends (B) to size from 1 × 6" cedar stock. NOTE: The grain runs horizontally on the sides and vertically on the ends.

2. Position the ends between the sides with the top edges flush. Drill pilot holes, and fasten with 6d finishing nails **(photo A).** Make sure the end pieces are oriented so the wood grain runs vertically.

3. Measure, mark and cut the bottom (C) to size, using a circular saw.

4. Draw a reference line down the middle of the bottom. Use a ½" spade bit to drill three drainage holes evenly spaced along the line.

5. Measure, mark and cut the feet (F) to size from ¾" cedar. Position the feet flush at the corners of the bottom piece and attach with 4d nails.

6. Draw reference lines on the inside faces of the side pieces, 1½" from the bottom edges.

7. With the box frame on its side, insert the bottom piece into the box, and tap into place until the bottom surface is flush with the reference lines. Drill pilot holes and drive 6d finish nails through the sides and ends to secure the bottom piece in place **(photo B).**

8. Measure, mark and cut the frame sides (D) and frame ends (E) to size from ¾" cedar, mitering the ends at 45°.

9. Position the frame pieces over the top of the planter box so the inside edges are flush with the inside surfaces of the box. Drill pilot holes and attach the frame pieces to the side and end pieces with 4d finishing nails. Lock-nail the miter joints with 4d finishing nails.

10. Recess all nail heads with a nail set, then finish as desired. Cedar will age naturally, but you can also seal it, as we did, with a clear wood preservative to maintain its original color.

TIP
You can prevent rot and extend the life of your planter by adding a plastic insert to hold the soil and plants.

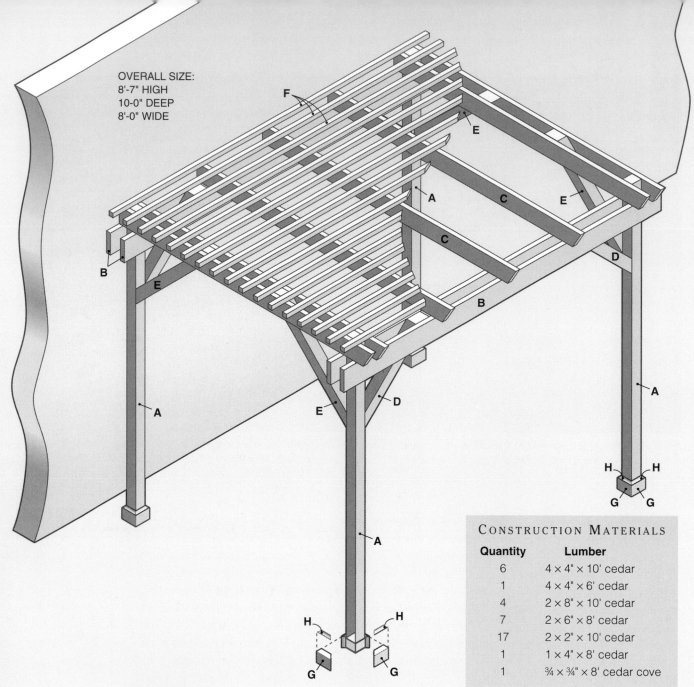

OVERALL SIZE:
8'-7" HIGH
10-0" DEEP
8'-0" WIDE

CONSTRUCTION MATERIALS

Quantity	Lumber
6	4 × 4" × 10' cedar
1	4 × 4" × 6' cedar
4	2 × 8" × 10' cedar
7	2 × 6" × 8' cedar
17	2 × 2" × 10' cedar
1	1 × 4" × 8' cedar
1	¾ × ¾" × 8' cedar cove

Arbor

Create a pleasant outdoor shelter.

Arbors provide a cozy feeling of enclosure without boxing you in. Sit back and enjoy the cool summer breeze in this simple structure, personalized with your wind chimes, bird feeders, banners or vines.

Cutting List

Key	Part	Dimension	Pcs.	Material
A	Corner posts	3½ × 3½ × 101½"	4	Cedar
B	Beam boards	1½ × 7¼ × 120"	4	Cedar
C	Rafters	1½ × 5½ × 96"	7	Cedar
D	End braces	3½ × 3½ × 34¼"	4	Cedar
E	Side braces	3½ × 3½ × 42"	4	Cedar
F	Slats	1½ × 1½ × 120"	17	Cedar
G	Post trim	¾ × 3½ × 5"	16	Cedar
H	Post molding	¾ × ¾ × 5"	16	Cedar

Supplies: ⅜ × 6" lag screws and washers (16); ½ × 7" carriage bolts, washers, and nuts (8); 2½" galvanized deck screws (200); 4 × 4" metal post anchors (4); galvanized metal rafter ties (6); 6d galvanized casing nails (12); 3d finishing nails (8).

Note: Measurements reflect the actual thickness of dimensional lumber.

Fasten the corner posts in the post anchor hardware with deck screws.

Use string and a line level and transfer the height of the beams to each corner post. Note temporary bracing on posts.

Directions: Arbor

Even though this arbor is structurally independent and not attached to your house, it's designed to be built next to a wall. If you want to build it away from your house, on a far corner of your deck, simply lengthen the rafters and angle-cut both ends.

LOCATE THE ARBOR.
When positioning the arbor, make sure the back posts are at least 6" from the house (see *Side Elevation*, page 88) to allow room for attaching the back beam boards. The corner posts should rest on joists. If necessary, add blocking between the joists at post locations for added support.

SET THE POSTS.
1. Mark the corner post locations on your deck (see *Elevations*, page 88). Position the post anchor hardware and attach to the decking with deck screws.
2. Measure, mark and cut the corner posts (A) to length. You may wish to cut the posts slightly longer than the final height to allow for leveling the beams and rafters.
3. Cut eight temporary braces, approximately 6' long, with a 45° angle on one end.
4. Set the posts in the post anchors and attach with deck screws **(photo A).** Use a level to ensure that the posts are plumb, and fasten in position by tacking two temporary braces to the deck and each post. Leave the temporary braces in place until the permanent braces are installed.
5. Mark the height of the beam boards on one corner post, using a combination square. Stretch a string between posts and use a line level to transfer this mark to the other corner posts **(photo B).**

Front Elevation

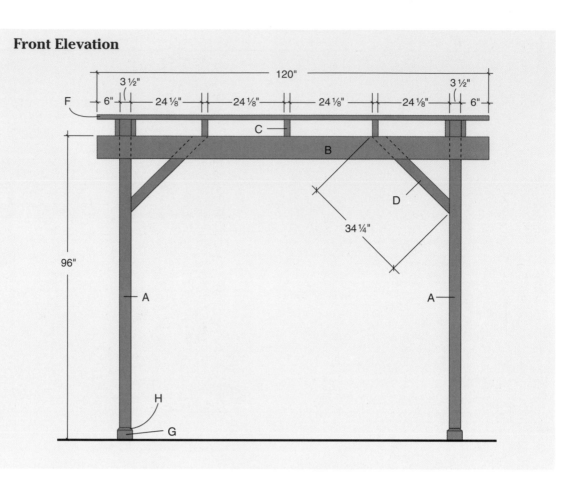

Side Elevation

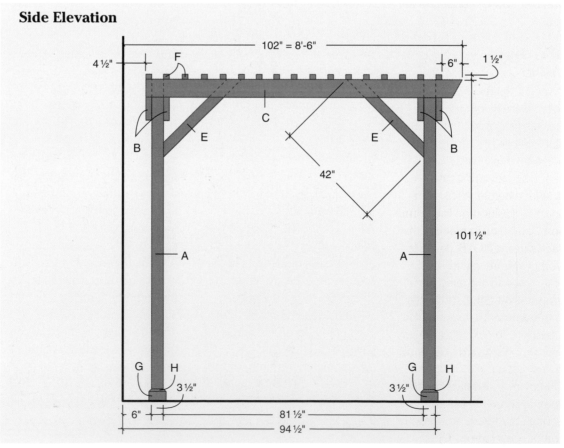

Detail A

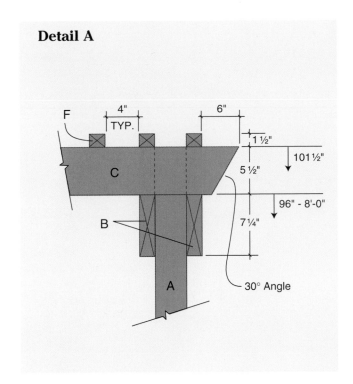

Drill two ½" holes through the beam boards and post for the carriage bolts.

INSTALL THE BEAMS.

The beams are installed between the posts, parallel to the house.

1. Measure, mark and cut the beam boards to length (see *Front Elevation*, page 88).

2. Stand the beam boards together on edge, ends flush. Measure and mark the outlines of the rafters on the top edges of the boards, using a combination square as a guide.

3. With a helper, hold each beam in position on the corner posts, and tack in place with deck screws. NOTE: If you're working alone, cut four 12"-long 2 × 4s, to use as temporary supports. Attach these pieces to the sides of the posts at the bottom edge of the beam position. Rest the beam boards on the supports.

4. Mark the carriage bolt locations, and drill ½" holes through the beam boards and corner posts **(photo C).**

Attach the inner rafters with galvanized rafter ties and deck screws.

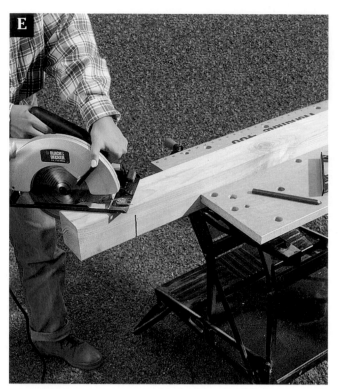

Use a circular saw to cut the 45° angles on the end and side braces.

To secure the top of each brace, drill and countersink a ¼" hole, insert a 6" lag screw, and tighten with a ratchet wrench.

5. Secure the beams to the corner posts with carriage bolts, washers and nuts.

INSTALL THE RAFTERS.
The rafters are installed perpendicular to the house, and overhang the front beam by 6". The front ends of the rafters are cut at a 30° angle (see *Detail A*, page 89).
1. Measure, mark and cut the rafters (C) to size, using a circular saw (see *Side Elevation*, page 88).
2. Set the rafters in position. Attach the outer rafters to the posts with deck screws. Attach the inner rafters to the beams, using metal rafter ties and deck screws **(photo D).**
OPTION: If you prefer a less visible method of attaching the inner rafters, toenail them with 16d galvanized nails.

3. Trim the posts to final height if necessary, using a reciprocating saw or a handsaw.

INSTALL THE BRACES.
The braces provide lateral support for the canopy. The end braces fit between the beams and the corner posts; the side braces fit between the rafters and the corner posts.
1. Cut the end braces (D) and the side braces (E) to size (see *Elevations*, page 88). Cut 45° angles on both ends with a circular saw **(photo E).**
2. Position an end brace between the beam boards, with the lower end tight against the post and the upper end flush with the top of the beam. Tack the brace into place with deck screws.
3. Drill a ¼" pilot hole through

the lower end of the brace into the post. Countersink the pilot hole ¼" deep with a 1" spade bit, and attach the brace with a lag screw.
4. To fasten the upper end of the brace to the beam, drill a ¼" pilot hole 5" deep. Countersink the hole ¼" deep with a 1" spade bit. Insert a lag screw and tighten with a ratchet wrench **(photo F).**
5. Use the same procedure to position and install the remaining braces.

INSTALL THE SLATS.
1. Measure, mark and cut the slats (F) to length.
2. Attach the back slat directly above the back beam board. Attach the remaining slats at 4" intervals, fastening them with deck screws **(photo G).**

G

Position slats at 4" intervals with a 6" overhang and attach by driving 2½" deck screws through the slats and into the rafters.

ADD THE
FINSHING TOUCHES.

1. Measure, mark and cut the post trim (G) and post molding (H) to length, with the ends mitered at 45°.

2. Fit and attach the trim to the posts with 6d galvanized casing nails **(photo H).** You may need to chisel out the back side of the trim to accommodate the post anchor screws.

3. Fit the molding and attach it tight to the posts with 3d finishing nails.

4. Though cedar is naturally resistant to decay and doesn't require an applied finish, you may want to use a coat of clear sealant-preservative for added protection and to preserve the original color of the wood.

H

Attach the post trim and molding with 16d galvanized nails.

Modifying a Deck Design

Modifying a plan lets you adapt your deck to unique situations.

Although the seven deck designs presented in this book offer a wide selection of styles and placements, it's possible that you'll want to modify a plan to fit the size or shape of your yard or just to suit your tastes. When you modify a design, you need to think about safety and structural integrity, the two most important features of your deck. This chapter will walk you through the most common modifications, showing you how to figure lumber dimensions so that your deck will be safe and durable.

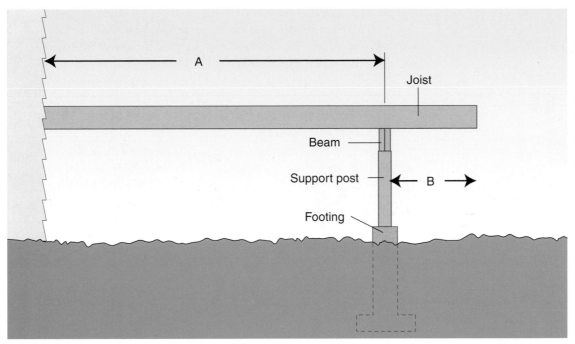

The length of the cantilever (B) must be taken into account when figuring beam and footing sizes. The cantilever should not be more than 2' unless special supports are added. A city plan inspector can advise you of the Code restrictions in your area.

The Parts of a Deck

The major structural parts of a deck are the *ledger, footings, posts, beams, joists, decking* and *stringers.* Once you're familiar with these parts, you can make sensible decisions about where extra support may be required and what kinds of modifications you can include without weakening your deck. (Remember to consult your local building inspector before modifying a deck design.)

In addition to a deck's structural members, decking boards are always a prominent feature. Your deck will probably also include *railings, balusters, risers, fascia boards* and a variety of less prominent parts.

Figuring Span Limits

To alter a design safely, you need to know the distance that a given board can travel between supports — known as the span limit. The larger the lumber, the greater the span

limit. In addition, some species of wood are stronger than others and have a greater span limit. Of the structural members, only the ledger is immune from span limits, since it is attached directly to the house with lag screws.

For any cantilevered deck plan, including those shown in this book, refer to the *Joist & Beam Chart,* page 111, to find minimum sizes for your deck's joists and beam. Use the post spacing and the length of the joists, A + B (A), to select acceptable joist and beam sizes from the chart.

If you lengthen a deck and add a second beam, use the post spacing and the distance from the inside beam to the rim joist to find joist and beam sizes. Remember that joists must be no more than 16" (OC) for decking boards that run perpendicular to the joists; 12" (OC) if the decking boards are installed diagonally.

Estimating Concrete

When mixing or ordering concrete for footings or a pad, you'll need a rough estimate of the concrete required. Mixes usually include estimated concrete needs for projects, as well as the yield per bag in cubic feet. Concrete companies measure per cubic yard.

When pouring 4' footings that are 12" in diameter, expect to use about 3¼ cu. ft. of concrete per footing, or about half that much for footings 8" in diameter. If local Code calls for flared bottoms, you will need to increase your estimate.

For a 4"-deep pad at the base of the stairs, figure ⅓ cu. ft. of concrete per sq. ft. of pad surface. A 4' × 5' pad would require 6.6 cu. ft. of concrete, or about ¼ cu. yd. (2 to 3 wheelbarrow loads).

Changing the Height of Your Deck

The plans in this book assume you are building on level ground and that the deck plan you choose is optimally suited to your home and yard. Of course, not all building sites are level and no yard is exactly like another. Your home may have a nonstandard doorway height or an uneven landscape. Or, you may simply choose to alter the height of the deck in the plan to suit your tastes.

When you change the height of the deck, you need to move the ledger, change the length of the posts and reevaluate post and footing sizes. You'll need to consider the need for railings, a step or stairs and post-to-beam braces. You may want to reconsider your joist placement (suspended from the side of the beam or resting on top). Finally, you may need to change either the length or the layout of the stairway, or both. You may even need to add a stairway or a landing that wasn't in the original design.

Increasing Deck Height

Raising a deck's height obviously means that the ledger will be higher and the posts will be longer. The posts may also need to be larger in thickness. If your deck is higher than 6', use 6×6 posts in place of 4×4 posts. Your inspector will probably also recommend enlarging the footings from 8" to 12" in diameter.

If you add posts to a ground-level deck and the height exceeds 30", you will need to add railings and stairs. Stairways with more than three risers require grippable railings as well. If your deck is over 12' high, braces are usually required for stability.

If you're adapting a ground-level design to an elevated installation, you'll probably want to extend the joists over the top of the beam to create a cantilever instead of hanging them with joist hangers on the beam's face.

Changes to the stairway design are covered later in this chapter.

Decreasing Deck Height

Decreasing the height of a deck obviously means that the ledger will be installed lower and the posts will be shorter. And it's possible that your lumber needs may decrease significantly. If the deck height is less than 30", you can safely eliminate the deck railings, and cross bracing won't be necessary.

Consult the section on stairways and landings for issues to consider when decreasing the deck height.

Adapting to Ground Level

When you adapt a deck design to a ground-level installation, you eliminate several construction steps and simplify others. You won't need railings, posts, stairways or landings — though you may need a single step if there's a slight rise. In place of posts, install direct-bearing hardware in the concrete footings while they are still wet. Once they are dry, fasten the beam directly to the

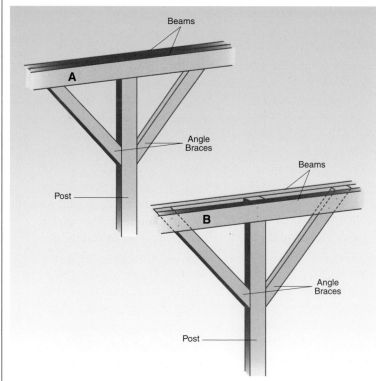

To reinforce an elevated deck built with a solid beam (A), install a Y-brace by attaching beveled 2 × 4s with lag screws to the sides of the post and the bottom of the beam. On a deck with a sandwich beam (B), use carriage bolts and slightly longer braces that can be mounted in between the two beam timbers.

hardware. The classic cantilever design — with the beam set back from the ends of the joists — is seldom used.

If you're building your deck very close to the ground, you may need to attach the ledger to the foundation wall rather than to the house's rim joist. To attach the ledger securely, drill pilot holes through the ledger and use the pilot holes to drill 3"-deep guide holes into the wall with a ⅝" masonry bit. Sink masonry sleeves into the wall. Then, position the ledger and attach it with lag screws driven through the ledger and into the masonry sleeves.

For a step leading to a ground-level deck, build a suspended step (pages 76 to 77).

Set direct-bearing hardware into footings while they are still wet. Use mason's strings to check the alignment.

Changing Deck Size

You may want to change the size of your deck to match the dimensions of building walls, to avoid windows or to work around other natural obstacles.

Increasing Deck Size
There are two ways to enlarge a deck. You can "widen" your deck by lengthening the joists and extend them out farther from the ledger. Or, you can add to the "length" of the deck by lengthening the ledger and increasing the number of joists.

If you're widening your deck, you'll want to know how far you can extend the joists beyond the beam. The cantilevered end of the joists (illustration, page 93) should typically extend no more than 2' past the beam, unless the

deck contains special supports.

If you want to extend your deck farther than this, you can move the beam out farther from the ledger and enlarge the size of the joists to allow for an increased span. To determine the proper joist and post sizes, use the *Joist & Beam Chart* on page 111.

Another way to provide support for an extended deck is to install a second, outer beam 2' or less from the deck's edge.

Lengthening the deck is usually a simpler alteration. It requires that you increase the length of the ledger and the beams, and that you add more joists.

Of course, when enlarging a deck you'll need to adjust the amount of decking and railing materials accordingly.

Decreasing Deck Size
It's a good deal easier to decrease the size of your deck than to increase it. When you decrease the size there are usually fewer Code issues to address. Since the overall load will be less, you don't have to worry about structural issues.

One strategy for making your deck smaller is to shorten the ledger and beam and reduce the number of joists. The alternative is to reduce the width of the deck by moving the beam closer to the house and reducing the length of the joists.

Your local lumberyard or home center can help you adjust the amount of decking and railing materials you will need.

Changing Deck Shape

Angled or curved decks are usually modifications of a square or rectangular deck design, with one or more corners trimmed.

Creating Angles

When adding an angle, it's often simplest to work with 45° angles. This allows you to work with common cuts (90° or 45°)

A

With a brace holding the joists in place, mark your deck for angled cuts.

B

Attach the rim joist along the angle by screwing it into the beveled ends of the inside joists using ⅜" lag screws. Then, reinforce the inside corners with adjustable angle brackets attached with joist-hanger nails.

and use skewed 45° joist hangers and other hardware that is readily available.

To create an angle, begin construction as though you are building a rectangular deck. After the joists are installed, use a chalk line to snap angled cutting lines across the joists. Attach a brace to the ends of the joists to ensure the spacing is correct **(photo A).**

Bevel-cut the ends of the joists at 45°, using a circular saw. Use a clamped board as a guide for the saw foot.

Cut and install the rim joists. At the angled corners, bevel-cut the ends of the rim joists at 45°. End-screw the rim joist in place **(photo B)** and reinforce the inside corners with adjustable angle brackets attached with joist-hanger nails.

Creating Curves

If you are building a curved deck, there are typically two design options: circular and irregular/elliptical.

Circular decks are laid out using simple geometry and a homemade, compasslike jig called a trammel.

Irregular or elliptical curves are usually found on low decks, since complex curves make it difficult to construct the railings required on elevated decks. These designs also work well for large decks, since the amount of overhang on the cantilever is relatively short compared to a circular curve.

To add a circular curve, cut joists slightly longer than their final length and attach them to the ledger and the beam. Add cross blocking between the two outside joists to ensure that they remain plumb.

Mark the joist spacing on a 1 × 4 brace, and tack it across the tops of the joists at the point where the deck curve begins. Measure the distance between the inside edges of the outside joists at each end of the deck. Then, divide this measurement in half to determine the radius of the curve. Mark the 1 × 4 brace to indicate the midpoint of the curve.

Build a trammel by anchoring one end of a long, straight 1 × 2 to the centerpoint of the curve, using a nail. (If the centerpoint lies between joists, attach a 1 × 4 brace across the joists to provide an anchor.) Measure along the arm of the trammel a distance equal to the curve radius and drill a hole. Insert a pencil in the hole and pivot the trammel around the centerpoint, marking the joists for angled cuts **(photo C).** Cut off the joists using a reciprocating saw **(photo D).**

For elliptical or irregular curves, the process for laying out the curve is different than for circular curves.

Start by nailing temporary vertical anchor boards to the outside joists at the ends of the curve. Position a long strip of flexible material, such as hardboard or paneling, inside the anchor boards. Then, push the strip to create the desired bow. Drive nails into the joists to hold it in position, then scribe cutting lines on the tops of the joists.

Use a speed square or protractor to determine the bevel angles for cutting the joists. Cut off each joist with a circular saw set to the proper bevel. On the outside joists where the curve begins, make 90° cuts.

The rim joist for an irregular or elliptical curve can be built using the same technique as for circular curves.

You can create the curved outer edge of the deck in one of two ways.

First, you can create a flexible kerfed rim joist, formed by making a series of thin vertical cuts (kerfs) across the inside face of the board and bending it to fit the curve **(photo E).**

Or, you can build a laminated rim joist by bending several layers of flexible plywood around the curve and joining the layers together using glue and screws. A laminated rim joist can stand alone, or it can provide backing for a more decorative fascia made of redwood or cedar.

When installing the decking on a deck with circular or ellipticle curves, begin by installing the decking for the square portion of the deck, then test-fit decking boards on the curved portion. If necessary, you can make minor adjustments in the spacing to avoid cutting very narrow decking boards at the end of the curve. When you're

satisfied with the layout, mark cutting lines on the underside of the boards with a pencil, following the edge of the rim joist **(photo F).** Once you've marked the boards, you can remove them and cut along the lines with a jig saw. Install them with deck screws. If needed, you can smooth the cut edges with a belt sander.

Nail the trammel to the centerpoint of the curve. Pivot the trammel like a compass to mark the joists for angled cuts.

Where the bevel angle is beyond the range of your circular saw, use a reciprocating saw to cut off the joists.

Blocking

Bend the curved joist around the bevel-cut ends of the joists, and attach them by driving deck screws. To prevent the joists from flexing as you install the rim joist, install blocking between the joists (inset).

Install decking for the square portion of the deck, then test-fit decking boards on the curved portion. Scribe cut lines on the underside of the boards.

Changing the Decking Pattern

The decking pattern determines the spacing and layout of the joists. A good rule to remember is that the ends of decking boards must be supported. When you change decking patterns, you need to reevaluate your joist spacing and layout. A straight decking pattern requires joists spaced 16" on center. A diagonal pattern requires a narrower joist space — typically 12" on center (chart, opposite page).

Similarly, borders and decking designs such as parquet, herringbone, checkerboard and other more complex patterns require additional support, such as double joists or blocking. For sturdy, flat decking, ⁵⁄₄ × 6" lumber has become the deck builder's board of choice. Avoid thinner lumber, which is more likely to twist or cup.

A straight decking pattern requires 16" on-center joist spacing.

A diagonal pattern requires that joists be spaced closer together, generally 12" on center, for extra support.

A parquet pattern requires double joists and blocking to provide surfaces for attaching the butted ends of the decking boards.

A border pattern requires trim joists to ensure that the ends of the boards are adequately supported.

Railing Style

Railings are required by Code on any deck over 30" high. Make sure your railings are firmly attached to the framing members of the deck with lag screws or carriage bolts. Never attach railing posts just to the face board.

Check local Building Codes for guidelines regarding railing construction. Most codes require that railings be at least 36" higher than the surface of the decking and that there be no more than 4" of open space below the railing or between balusters. Rail posts should be no more than 6' apart.

Vertical balusters with posts and rails are a good choice for houses with strong vertical lines. Horizontal railings, made of vertical posts, two or more horizontal rails and a railing cap, are often used on low, ranch-style homes.

Railing posts attached to the inside versus the outside of the rim joists create a neater, more enclosed look. The method of attachment is the same, but the timing is different. Posts positioned outside the rim joist are attached after the decking is laid **(photo A),** while posts positioned inside the rim joist are attached before the decking is laid **(photo B).** In either case, drill ¼" pilot holes through the post and into the rim joist. Then, attach the posts with lag screws.

When rail posts are surface-mounted to the inside edges of rim joists, they are attached before the decking is laid. Cross braces installed between joists provide extra reinforcement for the posts.

Decking Boards	Recommended Span
1 × 4 or ⁵⁄₄ × 6, laid straight	16"
1 × 4 or ⁵⁄₄ × 6, laid diagonal	12"
2 × 4 or 2 × 6, laid straight	16"
2 × 4 or 2 × 6, laid diagonal	12"
2 × 4, laid on edge	24"

Framing for Insets

Natural obstacles such as trees and boulders can greatly add interest to a deck. And quite often, it is less expensive and more interesting to build around a large obstacle than to remove it. Framing around a landscape feature does increase the difficulty of construction, but the benefits often justify the effort.

You can use the same framing methods to inset a pre-existing obstacle, or to create space for a decorative planter box, child's sandbox, brick barbecue or access hatch for utility fixtures, such as a water faucet, electrical outlet or air-conditioning compressor.

Before you start framing an inset, review your plan. Make certain your design provides support around any interrupted joists in the inset opening. If the inset interrupts one or two joists, frame both sides of the opening with double joists. If the opening is larger, you many need to install additional beams and posts around the opening for adequate support. If in doubt, consult your building inspector for specific requirements that apply to your situation.

Start by rough-framing the opening. Install double joists on each side of the opening. Install double headers between these joists. Then, install the interrupted joists between the double headers, the rim joist and ledger.

When creating a circle cutout for a tree or other landscape element, install angled nailing blocks between the joists and headers to provide additional support for the decking boards **(photo A).** When trimmed, decking boards may overhang support members by as much as 4" around an inset opening.

When building around a tree, make a cardboard template to draw a cutting line on the deck boards **(photo B).** Then, cut the decking boards along the template line, using a jig saw to trim the boards.

For access hatches, make sure you install cleats along the inside edge to support the cover.

Angled nailing blocks provide additional support for decking boards, which may overhang support members by up to 4" around an inset.

Use a cardboard template to mark decking boards for cutting. Leave at least 1' on all sides of a tree to provide space for growth.

Framing for Hot Tubs

Hot tubs are often built into a deck. In some cases, the tub is supported by the deck structure and is partially enclosed by a secondary platform. In other cases, it is fully inset into the deck and supported by a concrete pad on the ground below.

If the hot tub is to be supported by the deck itself, you should install an extra beam with posts and footings to provide additional support under the deck joists that are directly beneath the hot tub. In addition, the joists directly under the hot tub should be spaced no more than 12" apart. Structural requirements vary, depending on the size and estimated weight of your hot tub when filled with water, so consult your local building inspector for detailed instructions.

You will probably need to install new plumbing and electrical lines, so remember to consider the location of plumbing pipes and electrical cables, switches and access panels when designing your deck. For convenience, arrange to have the rough-in work for these utilities done before you install the decking boards.

Enclosing a hot tub with a secondary platform involves using framing lumber to build short vertical walls, using 2 × 4s for the top and bottom plate, and 2 × 2s spaced 16" apart for the vertical studs. Next, a floor platform built with 2 × 6 joists, spaced 16" on center is constructed on the wall structure.

Once the platform frame is completed, the vertical walls are covered with siding mater-

If your hot tub is supported by the deck structure, set the tub in place. Then, build 2 × 2 stud walls around the exposed sides. Measure, cut and install siding on the exposed walls.

Build platform steps to provide access to the platform, using siding materials to box in the risers. Code in your area may require a railing around the elevated platform.

ial **(photo A),** and the horizontal surface is covered with cedar or redwood decking boards.

The gap between the surface of the finished platform and the lip of the hot tub should be filled with caulk.

Finally, you will need to build platform steps leading up to the hot tub deck **(photo B).** Your local Code may also require that you install a protective railing around the elevated platform.

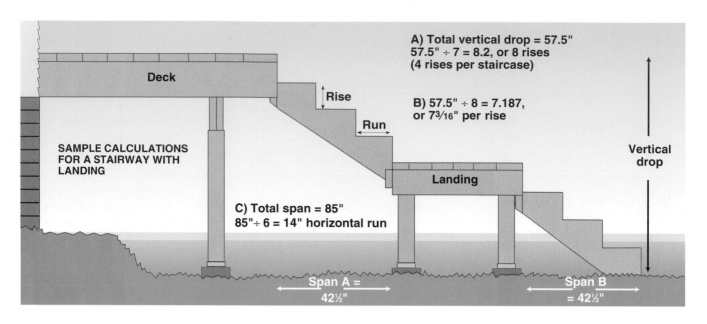

A) Total vertical drop = 57.5"
57.5" ÷ 7 = 8.2, or 8 rises
(4 rises per staircase)

B) 57.5" ÷ 8 = 7.187,
or 7³/₁₆" per rise

C) Total span = 85"
85" ÷ 6 = 14" horizontal run

Deck

Rise

Run

SAMPLE CALCULATIONS
FOR A STAIRWAY WITH
LANDING

Landing

Vertical
drop

Span A =
42½"

Span B
= 42½"

Changing Stairway Height

If you change the height or design of a deck, you may need to change the stairway layout as well. Elevating a deck, for example, may require that you construct a stairway that has two staircases joined by a landing (illustration, above). And even relatively small changes in a design may require that you alter the vertical *rise* and horizontal *run* of each step.

Vertical drop and horizontal span are the key variables when designing or changing a stairway. Vertical drop is the distance from the deck surface to the ground. The span is the horizontal distance from the deck's edge to the stairway's starting point on the ground. It is determined by whatever starting point you select. Once you know these variables, you can calculate the rise and run. Just remember this general rule: the span should be 40–60% greater than the vertical drop. For example, the span of a stairway with an 8' vertical drop should be between 11' 3" and 12' 10".

Stairway Basics

For safety and comfort, the components of a stairway must be built according to clearly prescribed guidelines. The rise, the vertical dimension of each step, must be between 6½" and 8". The run, the horizontal depth of each step, must be at least 9". The number of runs in a staircase is always one less than the number of rises. The combined sum of the step rise and run should be 18–20".

Steps that meet these guidelines are the most comfortable to use. Variation between the largest and smallest rise or run should be no more than ⅜".

Stair width must be at least 36", enabling two people to pass one another comfortably on the stairway.

Stringer spacing depends on the width of the stairs and the thickness of the treads, but should never exceed 36". A center stringer is recommended for any staircase with more than three steps. Very wide stairs may require more than one center stringer.

Finding the Horizontal Span & Vertical Drop

To determine the stairway's vertical drop, extend a straight, level 2 × 4 from the deck to a spot directly over the stairway's starting point on the ground. Measure the distance to the ground; this is the total vertical drop. NOTE: If the starting point is more than 10' from the deck, use a mason's string and line level to establish a reference point from which to measure.

The horizontal span is found by measuring the distance from the edge of the deck to the point directly over the starting point for the stairway. Remember that the span should be 40–60% greater than the vertical drop. If it's not, you'll need to adjust the starting point for the stairway until the ratio fits this range.

Lengthening or Shortening the Stairway

If you are altering the height of your deck, or if your building site is uneven, it's likely that you will need to lengthen or shorten your stairway.

Bear in mind that if the vertical drop is more than 12'—for example, if you are building a second-floor deck—a landing is required. In most cases it's best to construct the stairway so the upper and lower staircases are of equal length.

If you've decreased the deck height, you can shorten the stairway and bring the starting point closer to the deck.

To determine the number of step rises, divide the vertical drop by 7, rounding off fractions. Next, determine the exact height for each step rise by dividing the vertical drop by the number of rises.

Find the horizontal run for each step by dividing the span by the number of runs. If your stairway contains a landing, add the span for each of the staircases together, then divide this number by the number of runs. Remember that the number of runs in a staircase is always one less than the number of rises.

Once you have the exact rise and run for each step, it's an easy matter to use a framing square to lay out the steps on stringers.

Building a Stairway with a Landing

Building a stairway with a landing is one of the most challenging elements of deck building. The landing must be carefully positioned so that every step has the same rise and the same run. Accomplishing this often requires trial and

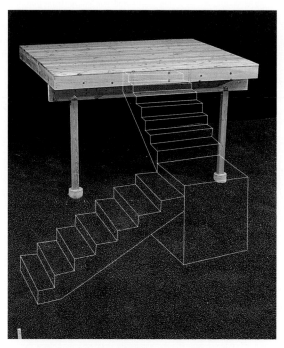

Visualize a stairway design that will fit your needs. Most stairways with landings are built with upper and lower staircases of equal length, although this is not required.

FOOTINGS & PADS

Footings and pads serve slightly different purposes, although they are at times interchangeable. A footing is typically poured into a form in the ground, reaching down several feet in regions where the ground freezes, and rising 2" or more above the ground to keep posts or stringers away from moisture.

If you want a concrete landing at the base of the stairs, pour a pad, typically 4–6" thick. Ask your inspector whether footings are required beneath the pad to withstand harsh winter weather.

revision. Start with a preliminary conception and expect to revise along the way.

Think of a landing as a large step that interrupts a tall stairway and you'll understand why its height must be set as precisely as the risers for the steps. If the height is not set properly, the adjoining steps will need unusually long or short risers, making the entire stairway difficult and precarious to use. Set the landing height with care and the landing will feel like a logical part of the stairway's progression.

You may choose to add a landing for either practical or aesthetic reasons or to comply with Code. But whatever the reason, think of the landing as a convenient place to change the direction of the stairway. You can use the change in di-

rection to fit your landscape or the lines of your house, or simply to suit your taste.

During the planning stage, divide the vertical drop into a series of equal rises and the horizontal span into a series of equal runs. On a stairway with a landing, add together the upper and lower staircase spans.

Landings should be at least 36" square, or as wide as the staircase. U-shaped stairways should have oversized landings, at least 1' wider than the combined staircase widths. Landings should be reinforced with diagonal cross braces between the support posts.

Support all stringers at ground level with concrete footings or a pad.

Adjust the landing frame until it appears square. To be certain, use a tape measure and confirm that the diagonals are of equal length.

When you are certain your landing frame is square, attach temporary braces across the corners to hold the landing's shape.

Building the Landing

For construction purposes, think of a landing as a small deck mounted on high posts. There are two implications worth bearing in mind. First, a landing's small surface area means you can build the landing frame on any level surface and then position it on the posts. Second, because of a landing's small area relative to its height, cross braces are necessary on at least two sides to ensure safety and stability.

Build the landing frame on a flat surface from 2×6 lumber. Join the corners with 3" deck screws. Then, check for square by measuring diagonally from each corner to the opposite corner **(photo A).** Adjust the frame until the diagonals are equal.

Find the position for the landing on the ground, then set the frame in position and adjust it for level **(photo B).** Drive stakes to mark locations for the landing posts, using a plumb bob as a guide. Install the footings and posts for the landing.

From the top of the deck, measure down a distance equal to the vertical drop for the upper staircase. Attach a 2×4 reference board across the deck posts at this height. Position a straightedge on the reference board and against the landing posts so it is level. Mark the posts at this height **(photo C).** Measure down a distance equal to the thickness of the decking boards, and mark reference lines to indicate where the top of the landing frame will rest.

Attach the landing frame to the posts at the reference lines. Make sure the landing is level before securing it **(photo D).** Cut off the posts flush with the top of the landing frame, using a reciprocating saw.

Remove the diagonal braces from the top of the landing frame, then cut and install joists. (For a diagonal decking pattern, space the joists every 12".) Attach the decking boards, and trim them to the edge of the frame.

For extra support and to help prevent sway, create permanent cross braces by attaching 2 × 4 boards diagonally from the bottoms of the posts to the inside of the landing frame. Brace at least two sides of the landing **(photo E).** Remove the temporary braces and stakes holding the posts.

Use a level and a 2 × 4 straightedge to mark the height of the landing frame on the posts.

After checking that the landing is level, use ⅝ × 3" lag screws to secure it with joist ties attached to the posts.

Attach permanent 2 × 4 cross braces diagonally on at least two sides of the landing from the bottoms of the posts to the inside of the landing frame.

To cut tread notches on center stringers, begin by using a circular saw and finish the cuts with a handsaw.

Set the staircase in place. Attach a 2 × 6 nailer to the landing to support the center stringer.

Building the Lower Staircase

To provide maximum support for the lower staircase, the stringers and bottom stair posts should rest on concrete footings rather than on a concrete pad. Insert a metal J-bolt in each footing while the concrete is wet, positioning each bolt so it will be offset about 2" from the stringer's edge. After the concrete dries, cut 2 × 4 cleats, drill holes in them, and attach them to the J-bolts with nuts.

Lay out and cut all stringers for both the upper and lower staircases (pages 102 to 103). For the center stringers only, cut notches where the treads will rest. Start the notches with a circular saw, then finish with a handsaw **(photo A).** Measure and cut all tread boards.

To assemble the lower staircase, use ¾" lag screws to attach angle brackets to the outer stringers where the treads will rest, then turn the stringers upside down and attach the treads with lag screws. The gap between tread boards should be no more than ⅜". Attach the center stringer by screwing through the treads.

Attach a 2 × 6 nailer to the landing to support the center stringer, then set the staircase in place, making sure the outside stringers are flush with the top of the decking **(photo B).** Use corner brackets and joist-hanger nails to anchor the stringers to the rim joist and nailer. Stabilize the bottoms of the stringers by nailing them to the footing cleats.

Building the Upper Staircase

Unlike the lower case, which is easier to assemble first and then set in place, the upper staircase is easily assembled in place.

Measure and cut a 2 × 6 nailer and attach it to the bottom of the rim joist, using mending plates **(photo A).** Measure and cut a 2 × 4 cleat to match the width of the upper staircase, including the stringers. Use lag screws to attach the cleat to the rim joist on the landing, flush with the tops of the joists **(photo B).**

Notch the bottoms of all stringers to fit around the cleat, and attach angle brackets on the stringers to support the treads.

Position the stringers so they rest on the landing cleat. Make sure the stringers are level and properly spaced, then toenail the bottoms of the stringers into the cleat, using galvanized 16d nails. At the top of the stair-

To support the center stringer, attach a 2 × 6 nailer to the rim joist with mending plates and screws.

case, use angle brackets to attach the outside stringers to the rim joist and the middle stringer to the nailer.

Measure, cut and position tread boards over the angle brackets, then attach them from below, using 1¼"-long lag

screws. Make sure each tread is level before you attach it **(photo C).** The gap between tread boards should be no more than ⅜". After completing the stairway, install railings.

Attach a 2 × 4 cleat to the rim joist on the landing, flush with the top of the joists. The notched bottoms of the stringers will fit around the cleat.

Begin attaching treads to the stringers, checking to make sure they are level. Maintain a ⅛" gap between the tread boards.

Building on a Steep Slope

The deck plans in this book assume you're building on level ground. But what if your yard is on a hillside? Building a deck on a steep slope is more complicated than building on level ground because of the physical demands of raising the deck frame, and because of the challenge of taking precise measurements before locating footings and cutting posts. The best approach involves modifying standard deck-building sequences.

The general idea when building on a steep slope is to start by building the outside frame and propping it on the ledger using a set of temporary posts, and only then determine the permanent locations for posts and footings. By modifying the conventional deck-building se-

quence you avoid the risk of digging and pouring footings only to find, after setting up the deck frame, that the footings are slightly off center.

Constructing & Installing a Temporary Support Beam

Once you've determined the size of the deck and attached the ledger, identify the approximate locations for the footings, according to your deck plans. Mark these locations with spray paint or stakes.

Next, position bases for temporary posts at least 2' away from the estimated footing locations, and level and anchor two 2 × 12 scraps on the ground to support the temporary posts.

Prop up the temporary posts

using 2 × 4 braces and stakes, and check the posts for plumb. Mark a cutoff line on each post by holding a long, straight 2 × 4 against the bottom of the ledger and the face of the post, and marking the post along the bottom edge of the 2 × 4. Cut off the posts at this height. A handsaw will work, although a reciprocating saw is ideal.

Construct a temporary support beam at least 2' longer than the width of your deck by face-nailing a pair of 2 × 4s together. Center the beam on top of the posts, and toenail it in place.

Building & Installing the Outer Frame

Build the outer frame of your deck according to your construction plans and attach joist hangers to the inside of the frame. With several helpers, lift the frame onto the temporary supports and carefully move it into a position against the ledger.

Endnail the side joists to the ends of the ledger. Then, reinforce the joint by installing angle brackets on the inside corners of the frame.

Make sure the frame is square by measuring the diagonals. If the measurements are not the same, adjust the frame on the temporary beam until it is square. Now, check the frame for level. If necessary, shim between the temporary beam and the side joists to level the frame. Toenail the frame to the temporary beam.

Locating & Pouring Footings

Use a plumb bob suspended from the deck frame to stake the exact locations for post footings on the ground. NOTE: Make sure the footing stakes correspond to the exact center of the posts, as indicated by your deck plans.

Dig and pour footing for each post, and insert J-bolts for post anchors while the concrete is still wet.

Attach post anchors to the footings, then check once more to make sure the deck frame is square and level. Adust the frame, if necessary.

Measure from the anchors to the bottom edge of the deck beam to determine the length for each post. When calculating the height of the posts, make sure to take into account the post-to-beam attachment method you've chosen.

Cutting Posts & Attaching the Beam

Cut the posts to length and attach them to the post anchors and to the beam.

For extra support and to help prevent sway, your inspector may advise you to brace the posts by attaching 2 × 4s diagonally from the bottom of the post to the inside surface of the deck frame. Toenail the braces to the post and deck frame using 16d galvanized nails.

You're now ready to remove the temporary supports, install the internal joists and complete your deck according to the original construction plan.

Lift the deck frame onto the ledger once the temporary posts and beam are in place. NOTE: On a very large or high deck, you may need to build the frame piece by piece on top of the temporary support.

Appendix

Glossary

Baluster — a vertical railing member.

Batterboards — temporary stake structures used for positioning layout strings.

Beam — the main horizontal support for the deck, usually made from a pair of 2×8s or 2×10s attached to the deck posts.

Blocking — short pieces of lumber cut from joist material and fastened between joists for reinforcement.

Cap — the topmost horizontal railing member.

Cantilever — a common construction method (employed in all of the deck plans in this book) that involves extending the joists beyond the beam or the beam beyond the posts. The maximum overhang is specified in the Building Code.

Corner-post deck — a construction method that incorporates posts at the outside corners of the deck with the joists attached to the face of the beams.

Decking — the floor boards of a deck (also known as deck boards).

End joists — the joists that are at each end of a series of parallel joists.

Face board — attractive wood, usually redwood or cedar, used to cover the rim joists and end joists.

Footing — a concrete pier that extends below the frost line and that bears the weight of the deck and any inset structures or furnishings.

Horizontal span — the horizontal distance a stairway covers.

Inset — an area of a deck that has been cut out to accommodate landscape features such as trees or to provide access to fixtures.

Joist — dimensional lumber, set on edge, that supports decking. Joists on attached decks hang between the ledger and rim joist.

Joist hanger — metal connecting pieces used to attach joists at right angles to ledger or header joists so that top edges are flush.

Ledger — a board, equal in size to the joists, that anchors the deck to the house and supports one end of the joists.

Notched post — a beam design that requires 6×6 posts notched at the post top to accommodate the full size of the beam.

Open step — a step composed of treads mounted between stair stringers without any risers.

Post — a vertical member that supports a deck, stairway or railing.

Post anchors — metal hardware for attaching deck posts to footings and raising the bottom of the post to keep it away from water. The end grain itself can be protected with sealer as added protection from rot.

Rim joist — a board fastened to the end of the joists, typically at the opposite end from the ledger. Rim joists attach to both ends of a freestanding deck.

Rise — the height of a step.

Riser — a board attached to the front of a step between treads.

Run — the length of a step.

Saddle beam — a beam design that uses metal fasteners to attach the beam directly to the tops of posts.

Sandwich beam — a beam design that incorporates a pair of beam timbers attached to either side of the post with carriage bolts.

Span limit — the distance a board can safely cross between supports.

Stair cleat — supports for treads that are attached to stair stringers.

Stair stringer — an inclined member that supports a stairway's treads. A stair stringer may be solid, with treads attached to cleats mounted on the inside face, or cut out, with treads resting on top of the cutouts.

Tread — the horizontal face of each step in a stairway, often composed of two 2×6" boards

Vertical drop — the vertical distance from the deck surface to the ground.

Index

Special Acknowledgments

P & M Cedar Products, Inc. Redding, CA
(530) 242-4600. Specializing in CedarPro™
sidings, knotty tongue-and-groove products,
and decking.

Canton Lumber, Brooklyn Park, MN
(612) 425-1400. Visit www.canton-lumber.com

Joist & Beam Size Chart

Joist Length		Post Spacing 4'	5'	6'	7'	8'	9'	10'
6'	Joist Size	2×6, 16" oc	2×6, 24" oc	2×6, 24" oc	2×6, 24" oc	2×6, 24" oc	2×6, 24" oc	2×6, 24" oc
	Beam Size	2-2×6	2-2×6	2-2×6	2-2×6	3-2×6 / 2-2×8	3-2×6 / 2-2×8	4-2×6 / 3-2×8
7'	Joist Size	2×6, 16" oc / 2×8, 24" oc	2×6, 16" oc / 2×8, 24" oc	2×6, 16" oc / 2×8, 24" oc	2×6, 16" oc / 2×8, 24" oc	2×6, 16" oc / 2×8, 24" oc	2×6, 16" oc / 2×8, 24" oc	2×6, 16" oc / 2×8, 24" oc
	Beam Size	2-2×6	2-2×6	2-2×6	3-2×6 / 2-2×8	3-2×6 / 2-2×8	4-2×6 / 3-2×8	3-2×8 / 2-2×10
8'	Joist Size	2×6, 16" oc / 2×8, 24" oc	2×6, 16" oc / 2×8, 24" oc	2×6, 16" oc / 2×8, 24" oc	2×6, 16" oc / 2×8, 24" oc	2×6, 16" oc / 2×8, 24" oc	2×6, 16" oc / 2×8, 24" oc	2×6, 16" oc / 2×8, 24" oc
	Beam Size	2-2×6	2-2×6	2-2×6	3-2×6 / 2-2×8	3-2×6 / 2-2×8	4-2×6 / 3-2×8	3-2×8 / 2-2×10
9'	Joist Size	2×8, 16" oc / 2×10, 24" oc	2×8, 16" oc / 2×10, 24" oc	2×8, 16" oc / 2×10, 24" oc	2×8, 16" oc / 2×10, 24" oc	2×8, 16" oc / 2×10, 24" oc	2×8, 16" oc / 2×10, 24" oc	2×8, 16" oc / 2×10, 24" oc
	Beam Size	2-2×8	2-2×8	2-2×8	2-2×8 / 2-2×10	3-2×8 / 2-2×10	3-2×8 / 2-2×10	3-2×8 / 3-2×10
10'	Joist Size	2×8, 16" oc / 2×10, 24" oc	2×8, 16" oc / 2×10, 24" oc	2×8, 16" oc / 2×10, 24" oc	2×8, 16" oc / 2×10, 24" oc	2×8, 16" oc / 2×10, 24" oc	2×8, 16" oc / 2×10, 24" oc	2×8, 16" oc / 2×10, 24" oc
	Beam Size	2-2×8	2-2×8	2-2×8	2-2×8 / 2-2×10	3-2×8 / 2-2×10	3-2×8 / 2-2×10	4-2×8 / 3-2×10
11'	Joist Size	2×8, 16" oc / 2×10, 24" oc	2×8, 16" oc / 2×10, 24" oc	2×8, 16" oc / 2×10, 24" oc	2×8, 16" oc / 2×10, 24" oc	2×8, 16" oc / 2×10, 24" oc	2×8, 16" oc / 2×10, 24" oc	2×8, 16" oc / 2×10, 24" oc
	Beam Size	2-2×8	2-2×8	2-2×8	2-2×8 / 2-2×10	3-2×8 / 2-2×10	3-2×8 / 2-2×10	4-2×8 / 3-2×10
12'	Joist Size	2×8, 12" oc / 2×10, 16" oc	2×8, 12" oc / 2×10, 16" oc	2×8, 12" oc / 2×10, 16" oc	2×8, 12" oc / 2×10, 16" oc	2×8, 12" oc / 2×10, 16" oc	2×8, 12" oc / 2×10, 16" oc	2×8, 12" oc / 2×10, 16" oc
	Beam Size	2-2×8	2-2×8	2-2×8	3-2×8 / 2-2×10	3-2×8 / 2-2×10	4-2×8 / 3-2×10	4-2×8 / 3-2×10
13'	Joist Size	2×10, 16" oc / 2×12, 24" oc	2×10, 16" oc / 2×12, 24" oc	2×10, 16" oc / 2×12, 24" oc	2×10, 16" oc / 2×12, 24" oc	2×10, 16" oc / 2×12, 24" oc	2×10, 16" oc / 2×12, 24" oc	2×10, 16" oc / 2×12, 24" oc
	Beam Size	2-2×10	2-2×10	2-2×10	2-2×10	2-2×10 / 2-2×12	3-2×10 / 2-2×12	3-2×10 / 2-2×12
14'	Joist Size	2×10, 16" oc	2×10, 16" oc	2×10, 16" oc	2×10, 16" oc	2×10, 16" oc	2×10, 16" oc	2×10, 16" oc
	Beam Size	2-2×10	2-2×10	2-2×10	2-2×10 / 2-2×12	3-2×10 / 2-2×12	3-2×10 / 2-2×12	3-2×10 / 3-2×12
15'	Joist Size	2×10, 12" oc / 2×12, 16" oc	2×10, 12" oc / 2×12, 16" oc	2×10, 12" oc / 2×12, 16" oc	2×10, 12" oc / 2×12, 16" oc	2×10, 12" oc / 2×12, 16" oc	2×10, 12" oc / 2×12, 16" oc	2×10, 12" oc / 2×12, 16" oc
	Beam Size	2-2×10	2-2×10	2-2×10	2-2×10 / 2-2×12	3-2×10 / 2-2×12	3-2×10 / 2-2×12	4-2×10 / 3-2×12
16'	Joist Size	2×12, 16" oc	2×12, 16" oc	2×12, 16" oc	2×12, 16" oc	2×12, 16" oc	2×12, 16" oc	2×12, 16" oc
	Beam Size	2-2×10	2-2×10	2-2×12	2-2×10 / 2-2×12	3-2×10 / 2-2×12	3-2×10 / 2-2×12	4-2×10 / 3-2×12